THE TOTALLY BRILLIANT SUPER PUZZLE BOOK

ARCTURUS

ARCTURUS

This edition published in 2013 by Arcturus Publishing Limited
26/27 Bickels Yard, 151–153 Bermondsey Street,
London SE1 3HA

Illustrated by Beccy Blake
Designed by Trudi Webb
Written by Lisa Regan
Edited by Samantha Noonan

ISBN: 978-1-84858-941-4
CH002505EN
Supplier 06, Date 0813, Print Run 2889

Printed in Singapore

WALKING THE DOG

Trudi is walking her dogs - or is it the other way round?
See if you can spot 10 differences between these two pictures.

GREEK ODYSSEY

Help Sophia through the Greek ruins to find her family.
Watch out for the sneaky snakes!

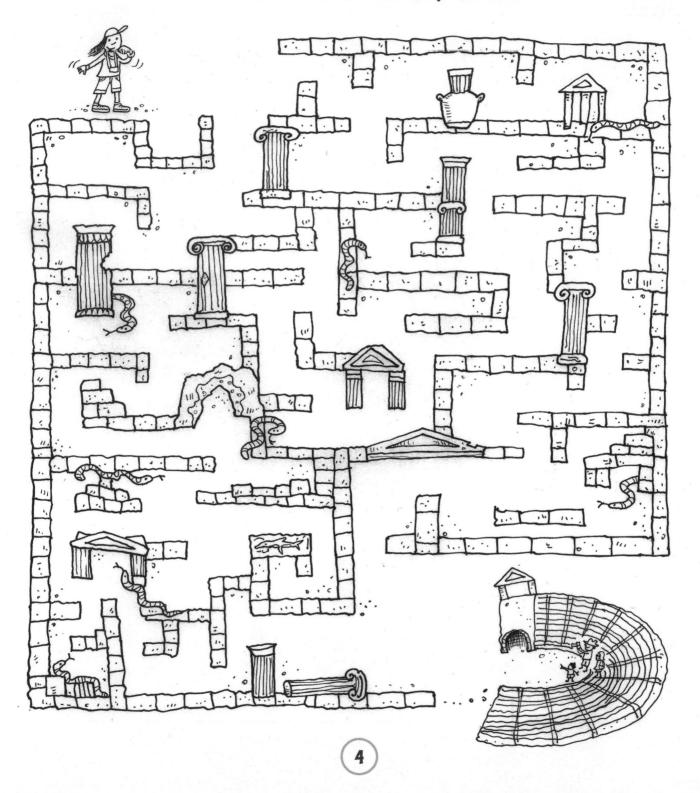

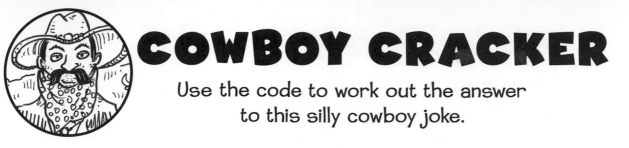

COWBOY CRACKER

Use the code to work out the answer
to this silly cowboy joke.

Why did the cowboy think his pony had a sore throat?

SLALOM SCORE

Add up the numbers for each canoe course to find out which boat was the quickest - the one with the lowest number.

SURPRISE!

The game warden has found some wildlife - but what
wildlife has crept up behind the warden?

SIX PACK

Help Rocket Girl to track down The Mighty Muscleman by finding a path using numbers that appear in the six times table.

MOUSE TRAP

Can you find the missing mice? The word MOUSE appears in the grid three times. Search up, down, across and diagonally.

M O S U E
O O U S E M U S E
U M O M O U S E M
U O M M O U S M O
M U U M O O S E U
O O O O M O S M S
U M O U S E M O S
S S S M U O U E
E E S O U S M
M S O E

9

DESTINATION UNKNOWN

The ticket office at Totally Brilliant Airways is in uproar! Can you match the torn tickets to make six capital cities?

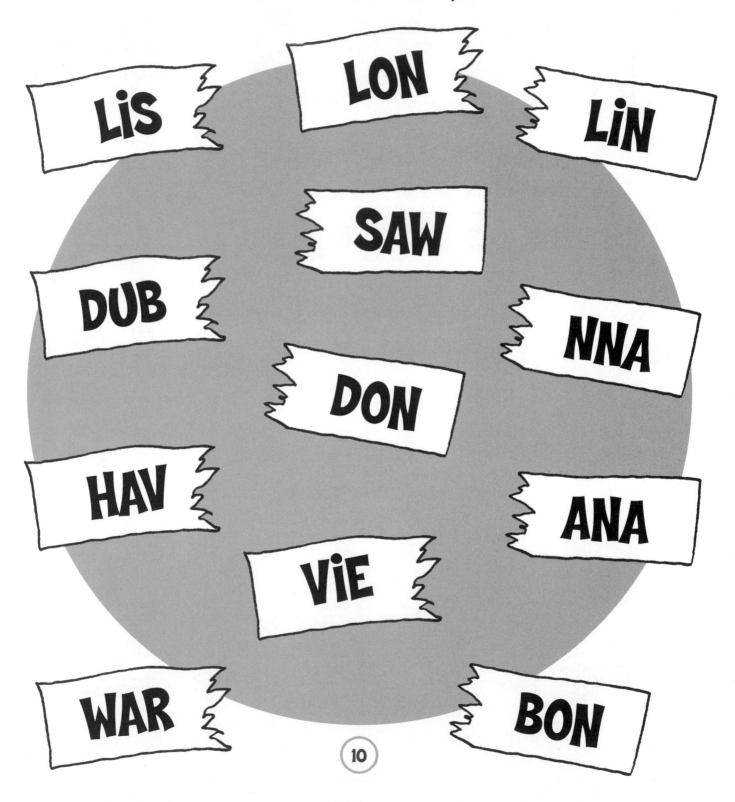

LIS

LON

LIN

SAW

DUB

NNA

DON

HAV

ANA

VIE

WAR

BON

RODEO RIDER

Which of the pieces finishes the jigsaw properly?

a b c d e

ON THE BALL

Use only the letters on balls you hit to spell out the name of a sport. There is a clue on the page to help you.

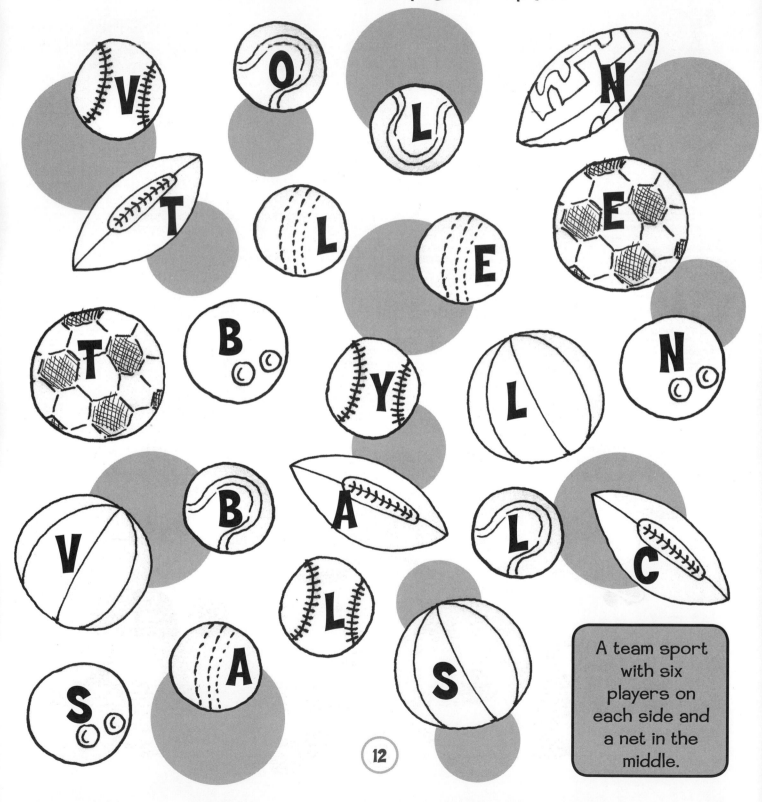

A team sport with six players on each side and a net in the middle.

PENGUIN PARADE

Each of these penguins has an identical twin, except one.
Which one is it?

A PRICKLY PROBLEM

Which of the pictures needs to replace the question mark
to finish the pattern properly?

PLAY TIME

Hammy the hamster is bored. Can you draw
some toys for him to play with?

TIME FOR A TRIP

Use the unusual clock to spell out two places that Johnny has visited. Follow the instructions carefully.

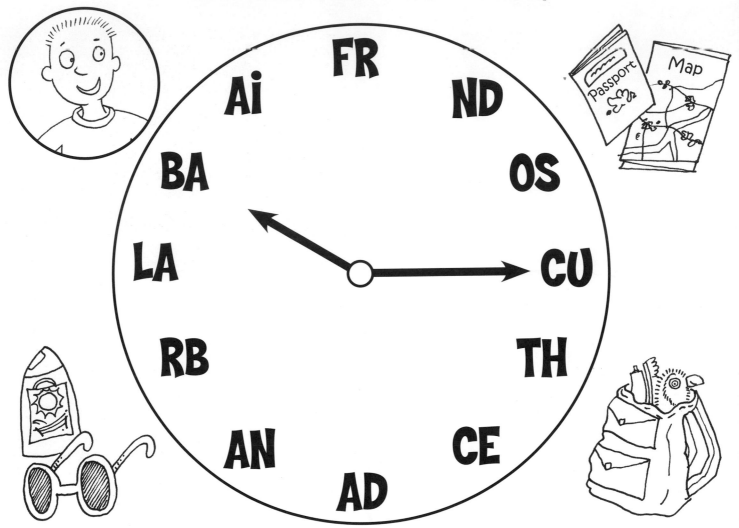

Write down the letters shown by the minute hand, then by the hour hand, for each time. Together, they will spell the places you are looking for. For example, quarter past ten = CUBA.

a   twenty past eleven
quarter to one

b   ten to eight
half past two

CROSS EYED

How many heart shapes can
you count in the picture altogether?

BULLSEYE

Add up the scores on each target to see who has scored the most points. Use the key to help you.

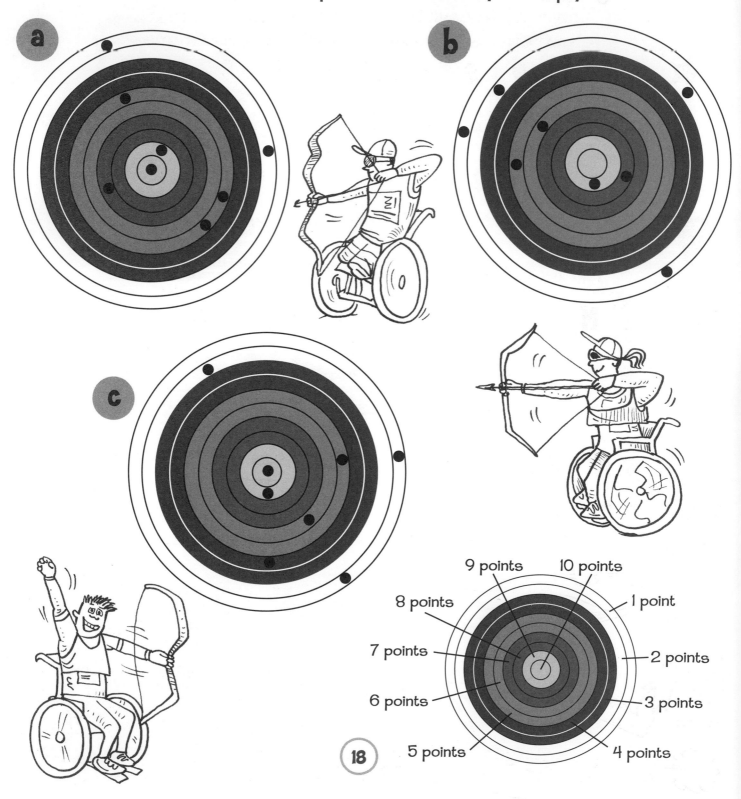

a

b

c

9 points   10 points

8 points   1 point

7 points   2 points

6 points   3 points

5 points   4 points

18

SUPERBAD

The Blue Comet is on the tail of another super villain! Shade every square containing the letters B, D or M and the remaining letters will spell the name of the evil baddie who must be stopped!

SETTING UP HOME

A badger's home is made up of underground tunnels, and is called a sett. In which order must Mrs Badger travel through the tunnels to collect sticks, then leaves, and take them to her babies?

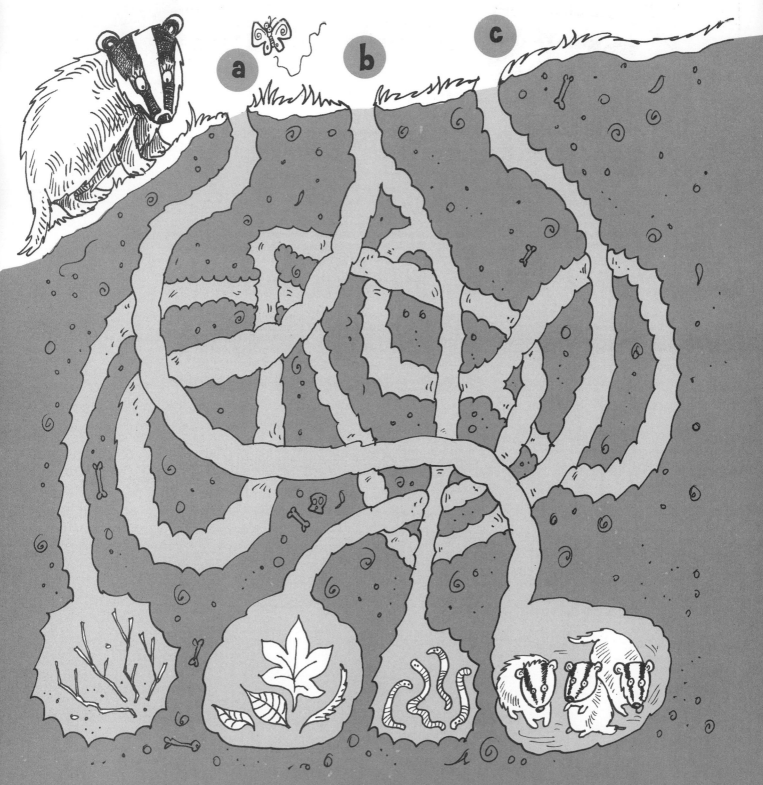

BEST IN SHOW

How many new words with three or more letters can you make from the letters below? One has been done to get you started.

PETS WIN PRIZES

PRINT

1. _____
2. _____
3. _____
4. _____
5. _____
6. _____
7. _____
8. _____
9. _____
10. _____
11. _____
12. _____
13. _____
14. _____
15. _____

SWEET TREATS

Yummy! Katie is on summer break and it's time for ice cream.
Find a path from the top to the bottom of the grid following the ice
creams in the order shown.

START

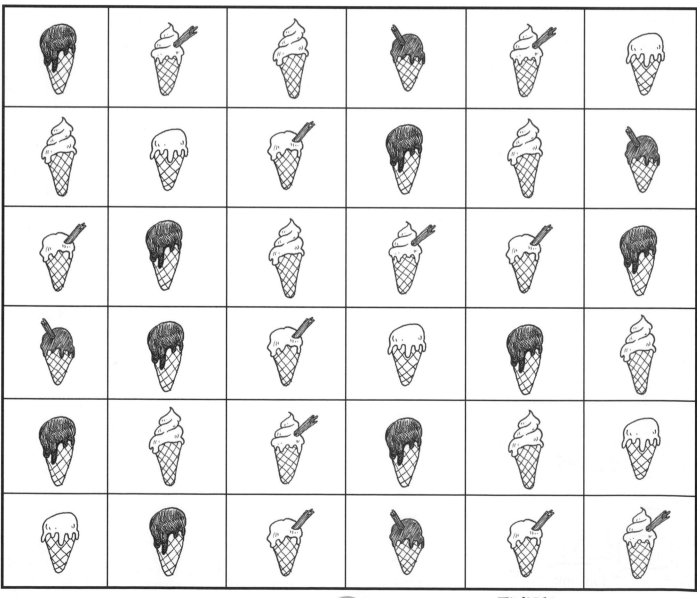

FINISH

HATS OFF

Who do you think this hat belongs to? Cowboy Cara or maybe Wild Jim McWestern? Draw the best cowboy or cowgirl you can imagine.

ALL TIME GREATS

Cross out every other letter on each race track, starting at the numbers. The answer in each lane will reveal the only five sports that have been in every summer Olympic games since 1896.

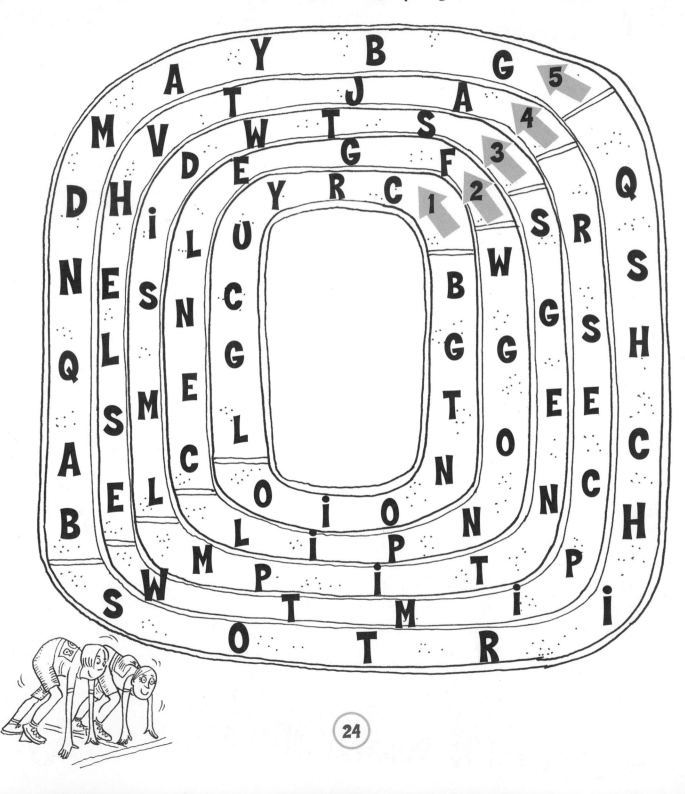

24

PERFECT PRIMATES

Primates are a group of animals that includes monkeys, apes and humans.
Find all the listed primates, including Norman, the nutty human!

MANDRILL
MARMOSET
BABOON
CHIMP
GIBBON
AYE-AYE

MONKEY
ORANGUTAN
MACAQUE
LEMUR
GORILLA
NORMAN

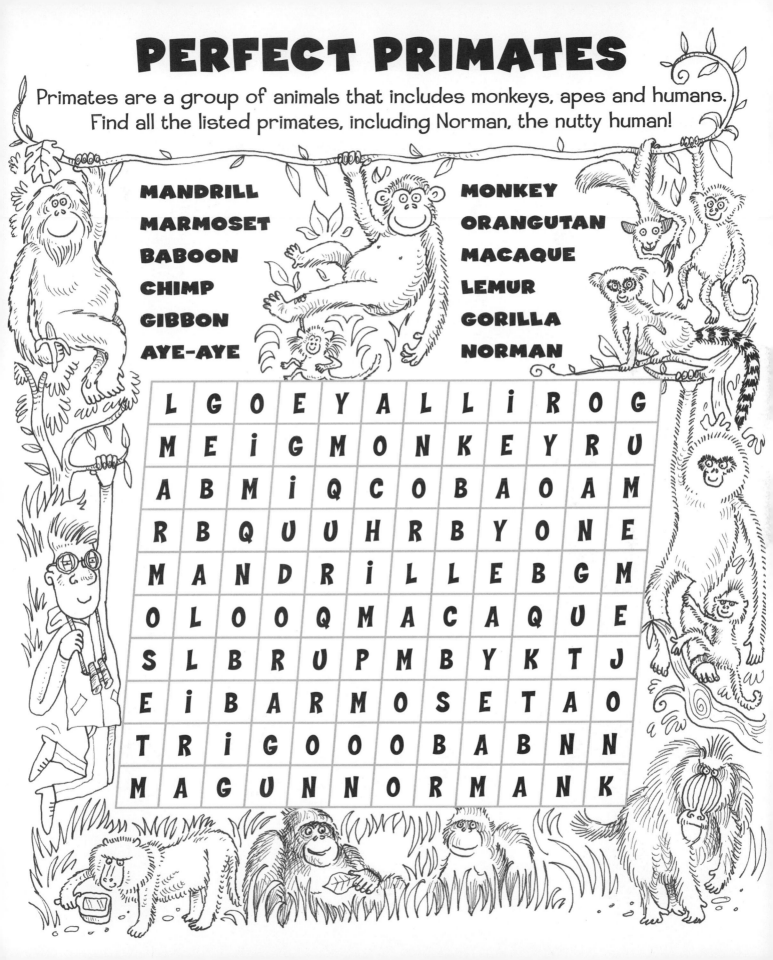

L	G	O	E	Y	A	L	L	i	R	O	G
M	E	i	G	M	O	N	K	E	Y	R	U
A	B	M	i	Q	C	O	B	A	O	A	M
R	B	Q	U	U	H	R	B	Y	O	N	E
M	A	N	D	R	i	L	L	E	B	G	M
O	L	O	O	Q	M	A	C	A	Q	U	E
S	L	B	R	U	P	M	B	Y	K	T	J
E	i	B	A	R	M	O	S	E	T	A	O
T	R	i	G	O	O	O	B	A	B	N	N
M	A	G	U	N	N	O	R	M	A	N	K

PET PANDEMONIUM

It's cleaning time at CitiPets but it has all gone a bit wrong! How many pets in the first picture are missing from the second picture?

WISH YOU WERE HERE

Design some postcards to send home from the best trips you can think of.

GREETINGS FROM

THE ULTIMATE DREAM DESTINATION!

SHERIFF'S SUDOKU

Help the Sheriff fill in the grid so that each row, column and mini-grid has one of each symbol.

SPORTS KIT

The kit room needs tidying so that everything is put into pairs.
What goes with what?

PAW PRINTS

Rearrange each set of letters to find out which animals made these paw prints.

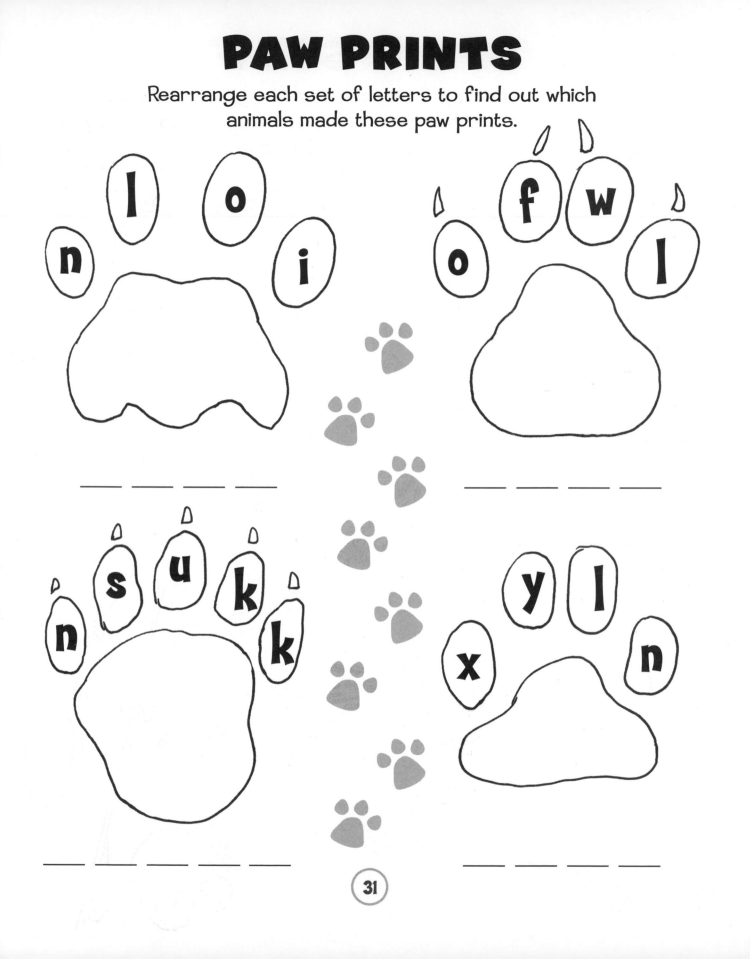

n l o i

o f w l

n s u k k

x y l n

COMIC STRIP

Put the pictures of Super Horace in the correct order to tell the story properly.

BRAIN TEASER

Use the clues to work out which person owns each pet, and what the animals are called.

	Cat	Gerbil	Pony
Carl			
Susie			
Grace			

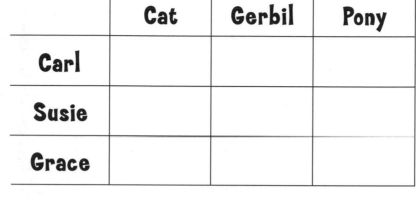

Susie doesn't own a gerbil.

Her pet isn't called Peppa.

The cat is owned by a girl.

Carl's pet is called Hector.

Grace is afraid of horses.

The largest pet is called Crystal.

Carl's pet is smaller than Grace's.

	Cat	Gerbil	Pony
Crystal			
Peppa			
Hector			

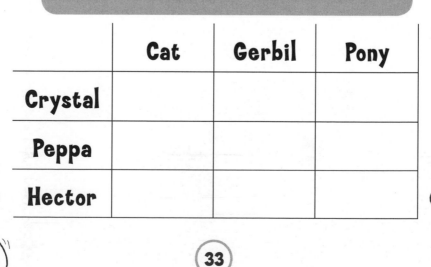

CHOCOHOLICS

Can you find one chocolate here that is not the same shape as any of the others?

SPOON SEARCH

How many spoons can you count in this Wild West picture?

BACK OF THE NET!

What sport is being played on this pitch? Draw some players
and their equipment - either real or made up!

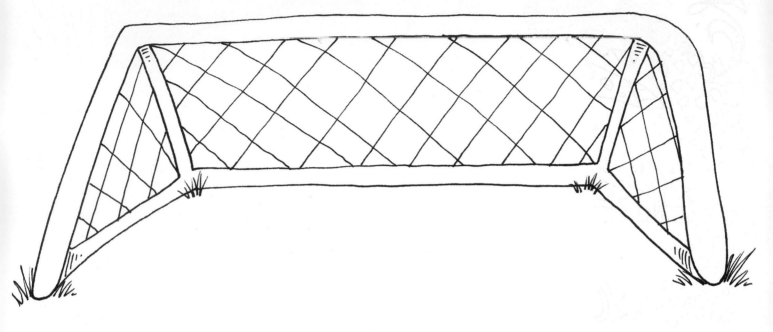

"C" CREATURES

How many living creatures can you think of that begin with the letter C? Well done if you can think of eight or more!

1. _____

2. _____

3. _____

4. _____

5. _____

6. _____

7. _____

8. _____

9. _____

10. _____

A COOL CLIMBER

The Great Gecko can climb walls like you wouldn't believe! Find a way up this glass building, using only numbers that are multiples of four.

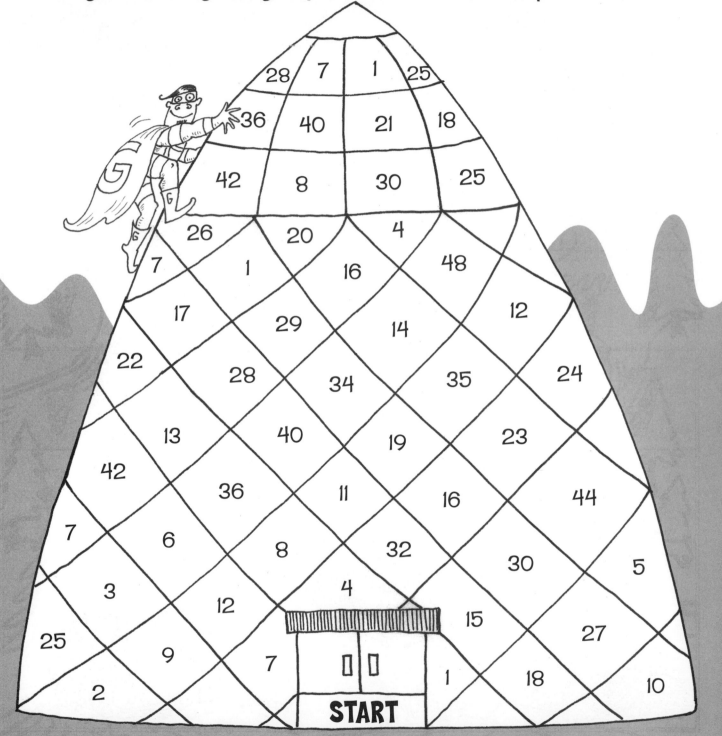

YOU CHOOSE

Oooh, it's hard to choose a pet when they're all so cute! Find the two guinea pigs here that are exactly the same.

IN A STATE

Use the clue letters to fit the US states in the correct places on the grid.
The circled letters will then spell out another state.

ALABAMA   NEW YORK

ARIZONA   MONTANA

FLORIDA   WYOMING

GEORGIA

QUICK ON THE DRAW

Look carefully at the mixed up picture. Draw each of the squares in the correct place on the grid to put the picture back together again.

CROSS OUT

Follow the instructions to find the answer to the joke.

Why did the golfer have an extra pair of socks?

in	because	sometimes	only	whenever
before	case	caddy	he	wanted
could	mostly	bad	got	lazy
a	crazy	fields	dirty	hole
in	grass	bunker	really	bird
useless	bottom	one	bat	plenty

1. Cross out words with five or more letters.
2. Get rid of any word that ends with Y.
3. Lose the words beginning with B.

SAFARI TRAIL

Find a way along the dusty paths to the safari lodge, making sure you pass each animal only once. You aren't allowed to drive on the same path twice!

SUPER WHO?

Who's this flying through the skies? You decide! Give the hero a name, a costume and his own special superpower.

A TRICKY QUESTION

It's difficult to decide what to call a pet! Look along every row to find one letter that appears in each name. Find all eight letters to spell the name of Cassie's horse.

Asha	Harry	Micah	Hunter	___
Jessie	Severus	Pepe	Ember	___
Rex	Trojan	Bryce	Sparky	___
Scrappy	Che	Scooter	Archer	___
Furby	Cutie	Puma	Hudson	___
Macklin	Laddie	Lennox	Clover	___
Neo	Ennis	Nelson	Ike	___
Storm	Carson	Skipper	Usher	___

TRAIN TREK

Study the timetable to help Richie work out
the answers to his questions.

PARIS - MILAN - ROME

Paris	departs	10:41	11:05	14:41	16:35	19:45
Milan	arrives	17:56	18:17	21:56	23:47	05:38
	departs	19:20	20:12	23:20	01:12	06:45
Rome	arrives	22:45	23:56	02:45	04:56	13:24

1. What time does the first train leave from Paris? _____

2. How long does it take to travel from Paris to Milan on the 14:41 train? _____

3. If Richie wants to arrive in Milan just before midnight, what time should he leave Paris? _____

4. Which is the slowest train from Paris to Milan? _____

5. How long will he have to wait in Milan if he wants to go from Paris to Rome at 11:05? _____

SAY WHAT?

Use the code key to work out what on earth
this cowboy is talking about!

SADDLE   HIT   WORK   END   HORSE   ON   MY   BONE

IT'S   UP   AND   TAIL   THE   COW   TRAIL

Saddle   Up   And

Hit   The   Tral

EXTREME THRILLS

As the sun sets on the mountains, look carefully to see which of these snowboarder silhouettes exactly matches the main picture.

STINKY SUMS

Fill in the number pyramid on the dung beetle balls to find out how many tons of food a wild African elephant can eat every year!

To fill in the numbers, add two circles that are side by side, and write the answer in the circle above them.
One has been done to show you how: 3 + 11 = 14

ON THE MOVE

Follow the lines from the Mighty Mo's hands to rearrange the letters.
When they're in the right order, they will spell her uncanny superpower!

COLLARED

How many dog collars are there scattered on this page?

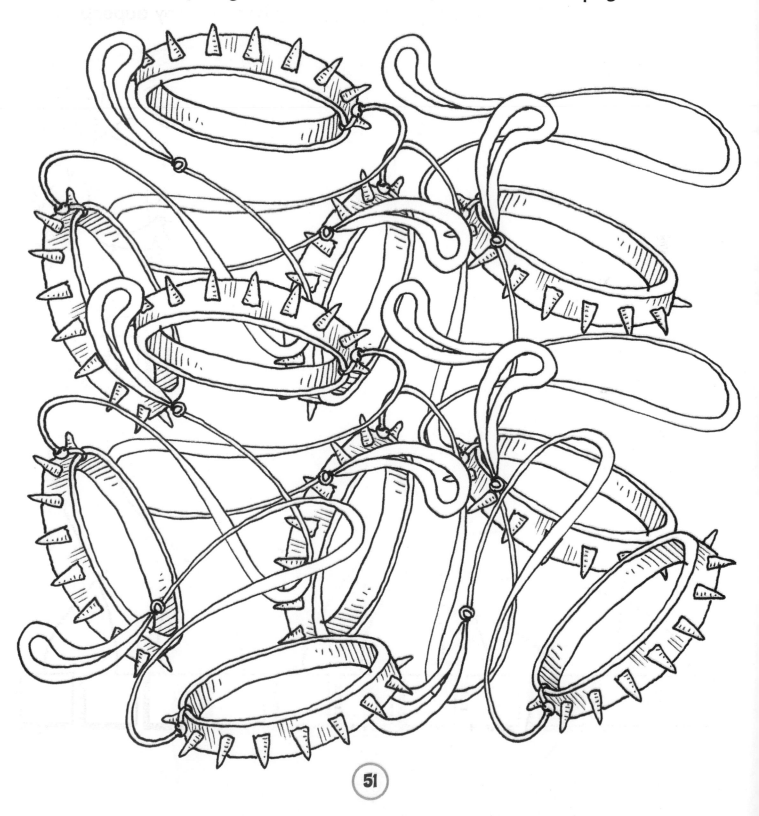

ROOM WITH A VIEW

What would you see out of your hotel window on your dream trip?

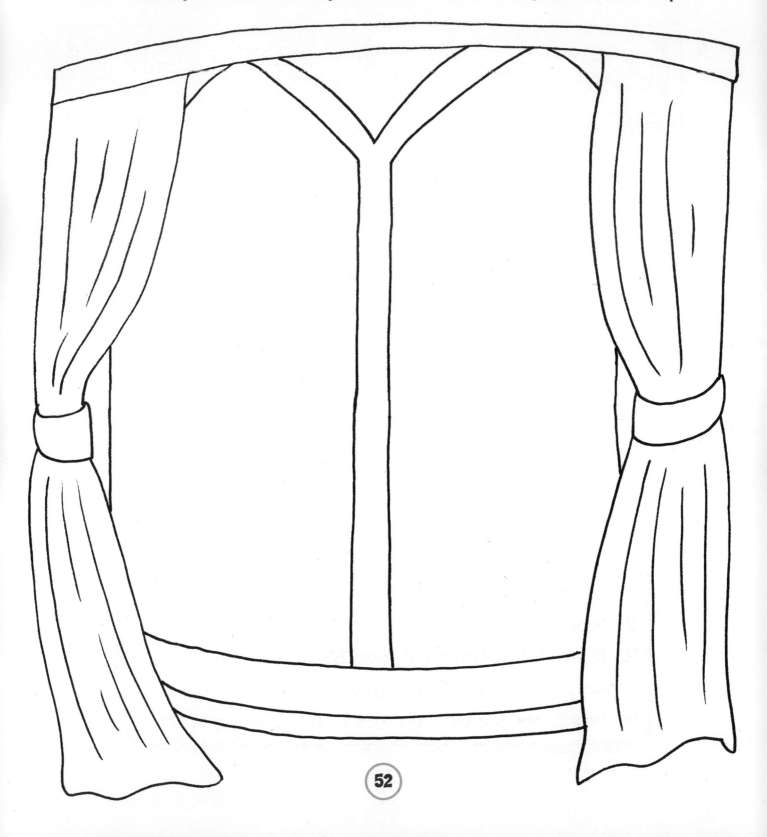

THE WILD WEST

Use the map of Bonanza City to answer the questions below.

1. In which square is the Sheriff's office?
2. What is for sale in E1?
3. If you follow the road from B3 to A4, what do you pass on your right?
4. Which square can you visit to buy a new saddle?

BOUNCE AROUND

Bounce from one ball to the next, following them in the direction of the arrows, and in this order:

1. 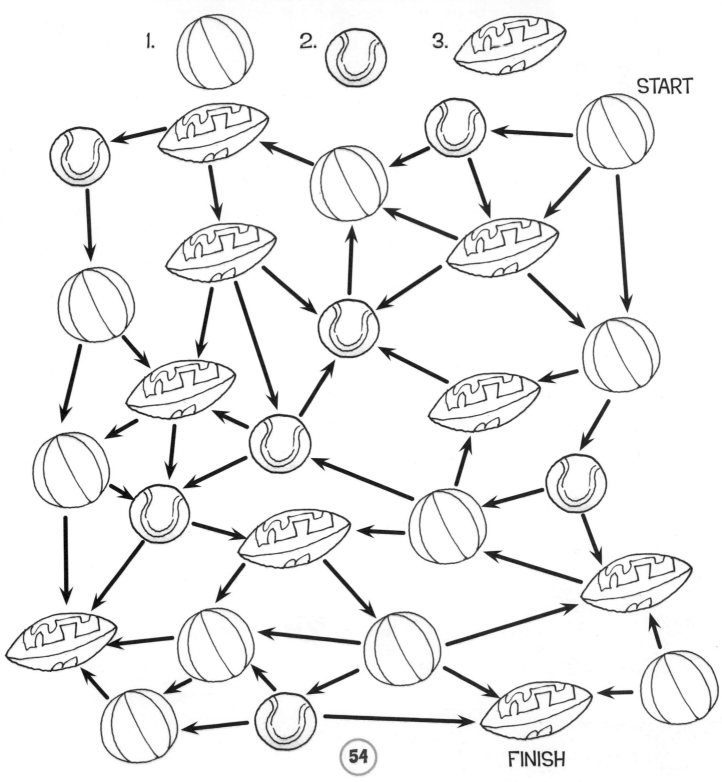 2. 3.

START

54

FINISH

CRITTER LITTERS

A set of babies born at the same time is called a litter.
Link each mother to her babies, passing through the sum that
gives the correct number for each litter.

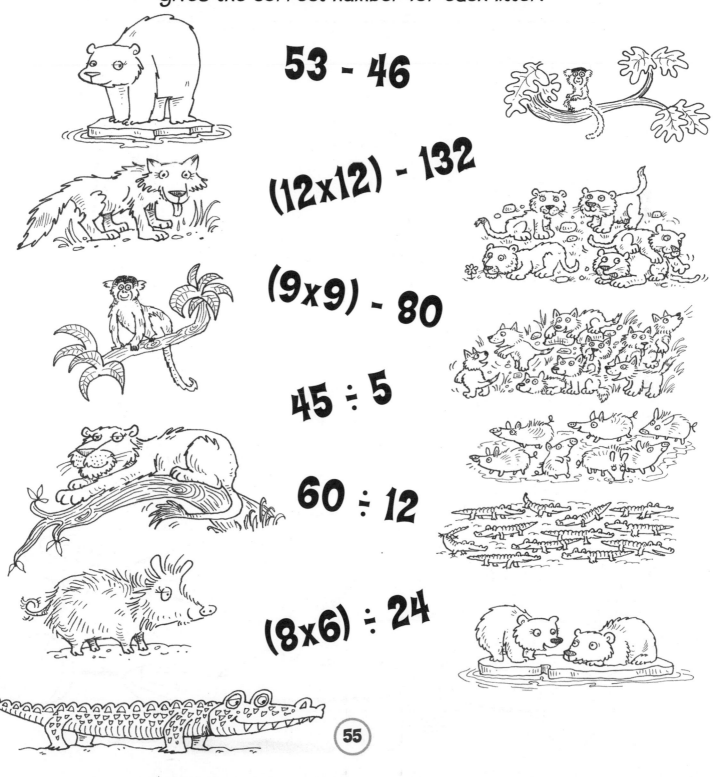

53 - 46

(12x12) - 132

(9x9) - 80

45 ÷ 5

60 ÷ 12

(8x6) ÷ 24

FLYING HIGH

Rita von Clapp is trapped on the balcony of the skyscraper!
Figure out which of the smaller pictures is the view Astrogirl
has as she flies over the city to rescue her.

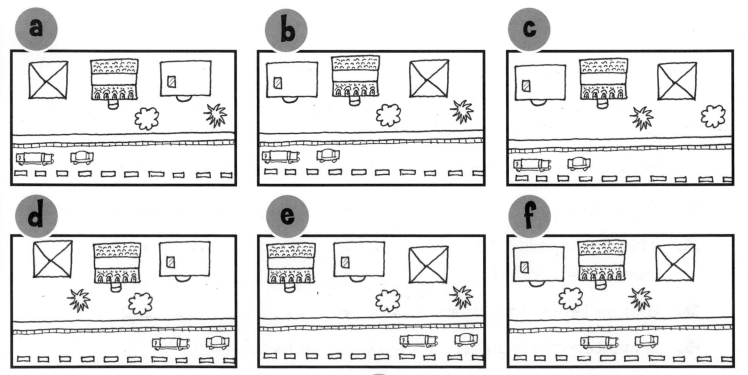

PET PUZZLER

Work out which clue describes each pet and write the number in the right square. All of the rows, columns and diagonals should add up to 15.

1. A pet with gills

2. This pet carries its own home around

3. Can be tabby or ginger

4. A master of disguise

5. A pet with no legs

6. This pet needs lots of walks

7. It might talk to you!

8. A squeaky creature

9. It has long ears and a twitchy nose

CAUGHT ON CAMERA

Look carefully at Suki's photo of the pool
to find each of the people circled below.

BEHIND BARS

Crack the number code to help Lola Starr get her true love out of jail.

1. 55 ÷ 11
2. 75 - 68
3. 3 x 3
4. 150 ÷ 50

ANYONE FOR TENNIS?

Can you find the word BALL hidden just once in the grid?

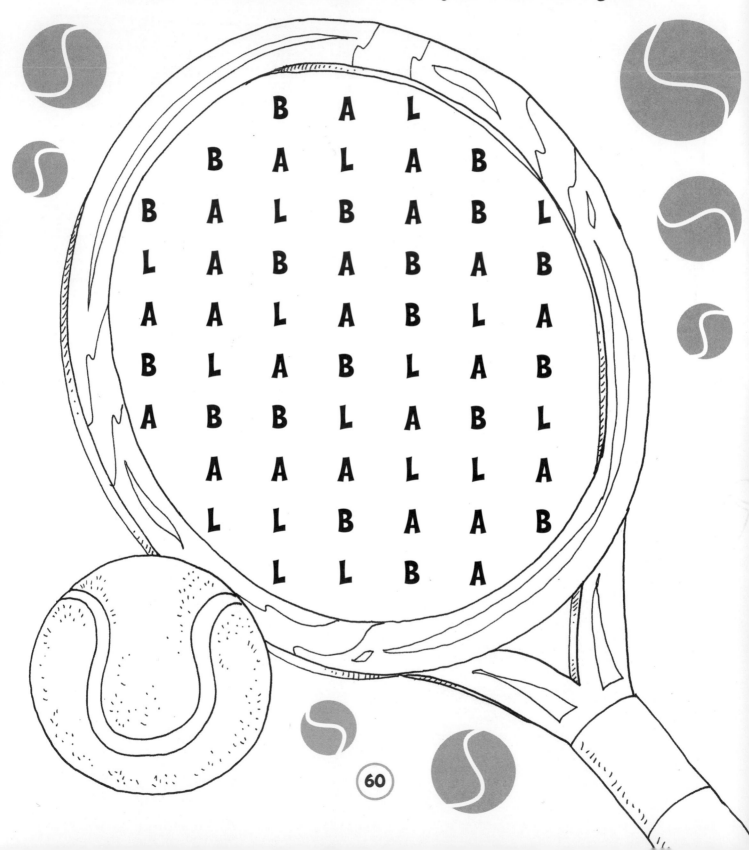

```
    B  A  L  L
  B  A  L  A  B
B  A  L  B  A  B  L
L  A  B  A  B  A  B
A  A  L  A  B  L  A
B  L  A  B  L  A  B
A  B  B  L  A  B  L
   A  A  A  L  L  A
   L  L  B  A  A  B
      L  L  B  A
```

TRAIL FINDER

Draw who - and what - you think has made these footprints.

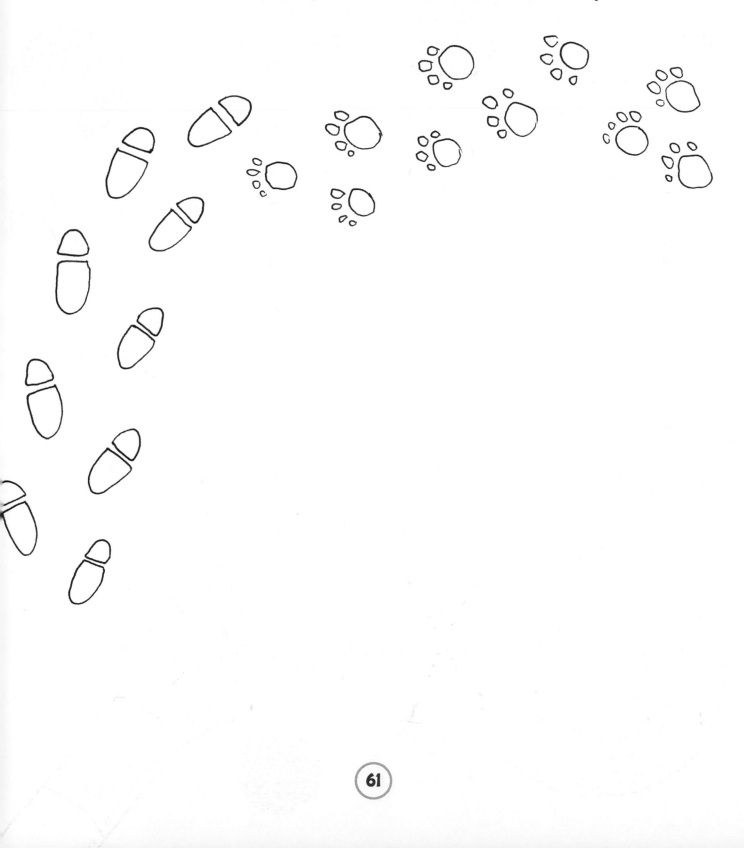

SUPER TROOPER

Use the grid references to write down the correct letters.
They will spell out what Trooper X's super power is.

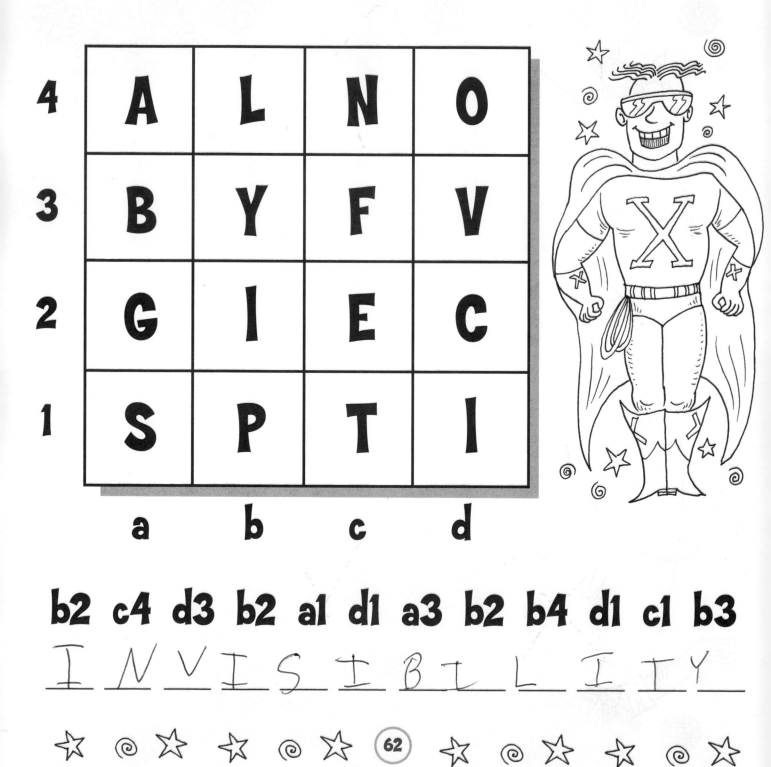

	a	b	c	d
4	A	L	N	O
3	B	Y	F	V
2	G	I	E	C
1	S	P	T	I

b2 c4 d3 b2 a1 d1 a3 b2 b4 d1 c1 b3

I N V I S I B I L I T Y

FLY AWAY HOME

Follow each bird to find out who owns each one.

LOST LUGGAGE

Help the baggage handlers at Totally Brilliant
airport find the correct suitcase for Mrs Rumpleton.

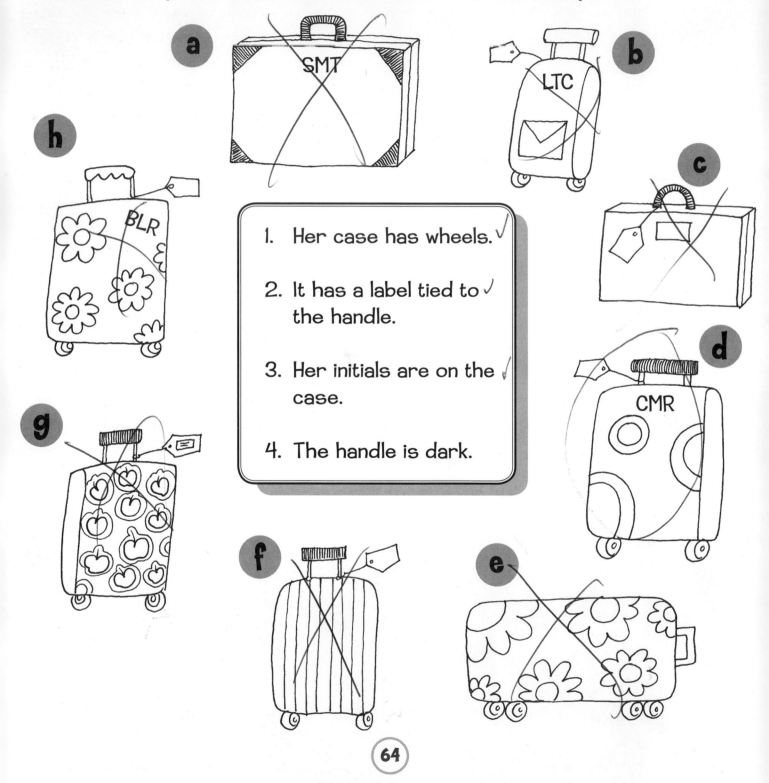

a — SMT

b — LTC

h — BLR

c

d — CMR

g

f

e

1. Her case has wheels. ✓

2. It has a label tied to ✓
   the handle.

3. Her initials are on the ✓
   case.

4. The handle is dark.

64

WAGON WHEELS

Use the letters on each wheel to spell six Wild West words.

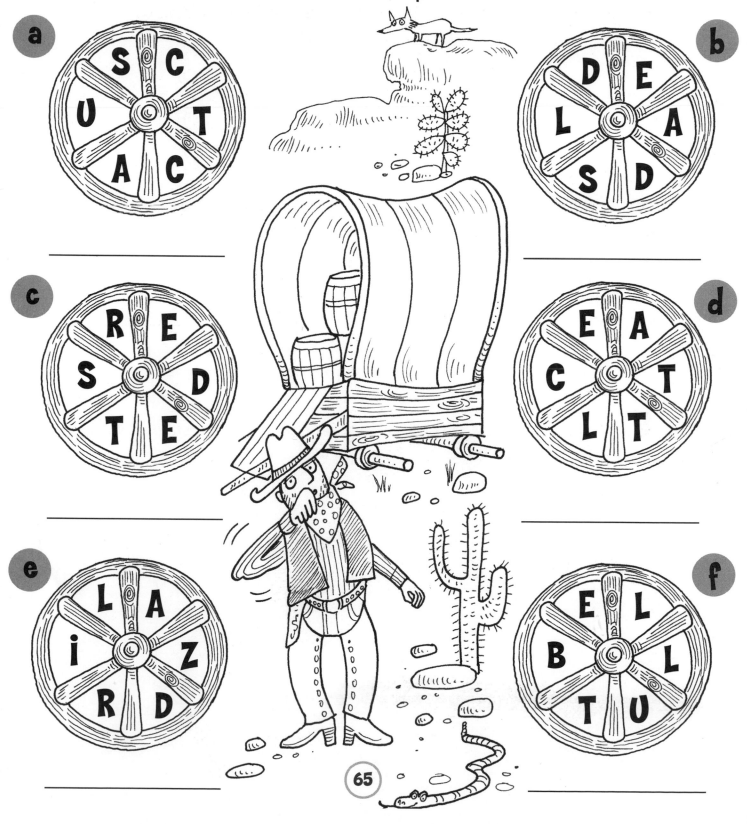

a S C T A C U

b D E A D S L

c R E D T E S

d E A T T L C

e L A Z R D i

f E L L U T B

SLAM DUNK

Alley-oop like a pro and guide the ball through the net maze!

LEAPING LEMURS!

Four of these lemurs are exactly the same. Can you see which ones?

SUPER SPELLINGS

How many words can you make from the letters below?
One has been done to help you.

SILVER SORCERESS

1. river
2. _____
3. _____
4. _____
5. _____
6. _____
7. _____
8. _____

9. _____
10. _____
11. _____
12. _____
13. _____
14. _____
15. _____
16. _____

TROPICAL TANK

This fish tank needs something in it. Can you draw some fabulous fish, and add some furniture for them to swim around?

CYPRUS SUDOKU

Fill in the blanks using the letters CYPRUS, in any order, so that every row, column and mini-grid contains each letter only once.

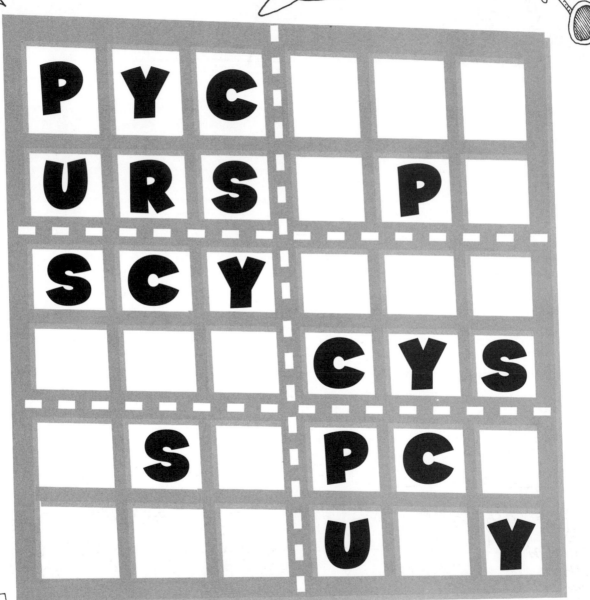

AMBUSHED!

Big 'Tone' Telford has been caught in the mountain pass by Wild Mikey Armitage and his gang. Can you find ten coins hidden in the scene?

PARK LIFE

Read the map and use the grid references to help you answer the questions about the sports park.

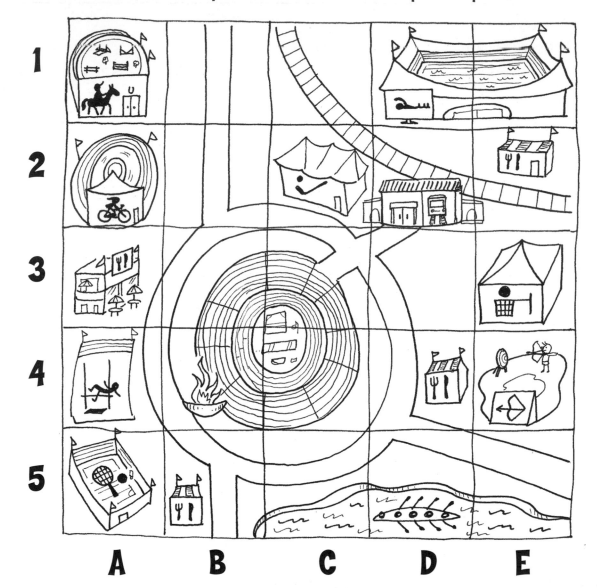

1 2 3 4 5

A B C D E

1. In which square is the train station?

2. What sport can you see in E4?

3. Where is the closest place to eat if you have watched the cycling?

4. Which of these does not have an entrance to the main stadium: C3, B5, C2 or B2?

5. What is taking place in A5?

6. If you want to watch the rowing, should you head to D1 or D5?

CUTE CUBS

Which of these cheeky cheetahs is different from the rest?

ON THE RUN

Start at the bomb and follow the letters to find six things a superhero wears. The leftover letters will spell the runaway villain's name.

NETTED

Study the two pictures to see which three fish from the top picture have been caught and taken to a new home.

RIDING HIGH

How many times can you find the word ALPS hidden in the grid?

```
L   L   A   P   S
A   A   L   P   A   P
P   P   S   L   A   A
A   A   P   S   P   A   L
L   L   A   L   S   S   P
P   P   L   A   L   L   S
    S   S   A   L   A   P
A   A   P   P   S   P   S
L   L   S   A   L   P   S
S   S   L   A   P   S   A
```

DRESS TO IMPRESS

Decorate this Native American headdress so it is fit for a chief.

STICK WITH IT

How many hockey sticks are there in this muddle?

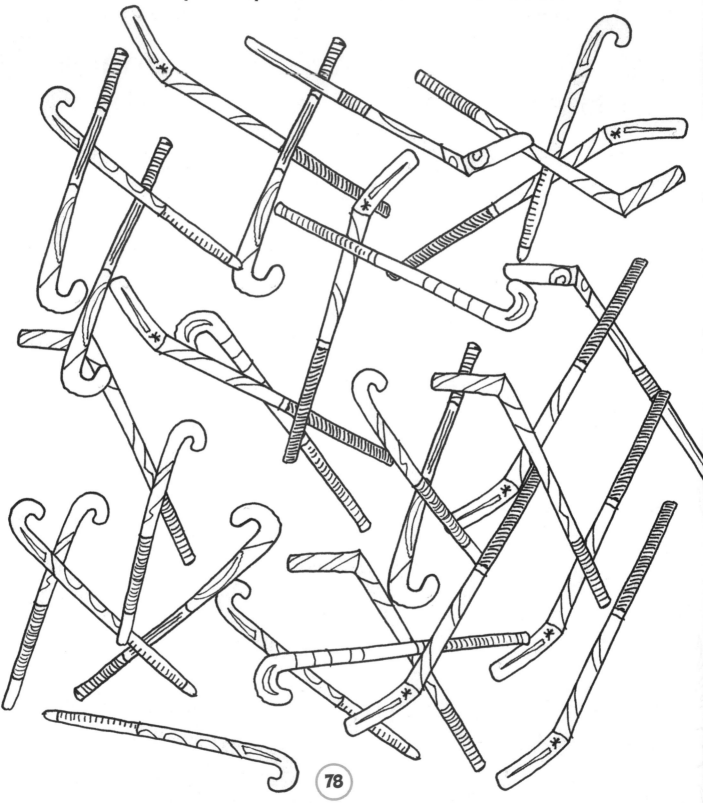

SSSSSSILLY SSSSSSTUFF

Shade in all the squares containing S, E and D.
The remaining letters will spell the answer to the joke.

What happened to the snake that swallowed a set of keys?

S	E	E	D	S	D	E	S	S	E
D	S	i	D	E	S	E	E	D	S
E	E	D	E	S	S	T	D	E	S
S	E	D	S	E	D	D	E	E	S
D	G	E	E	O	S	E	D	E	D
E	D	S	E	D	S	E	E	T	S
S	E	D	D	E	S	D	S	D	E
L	E	D	O	C	E	E	K	E	D
S	S	J	D	D	E	A	E	S	W
D	E	S	D	S	D	E	S	S	D	E	S

_____

SUPER SHOOTERS

Use the letters only from the guns shooting to the left to find out what Krall the Conqueror's super power is.

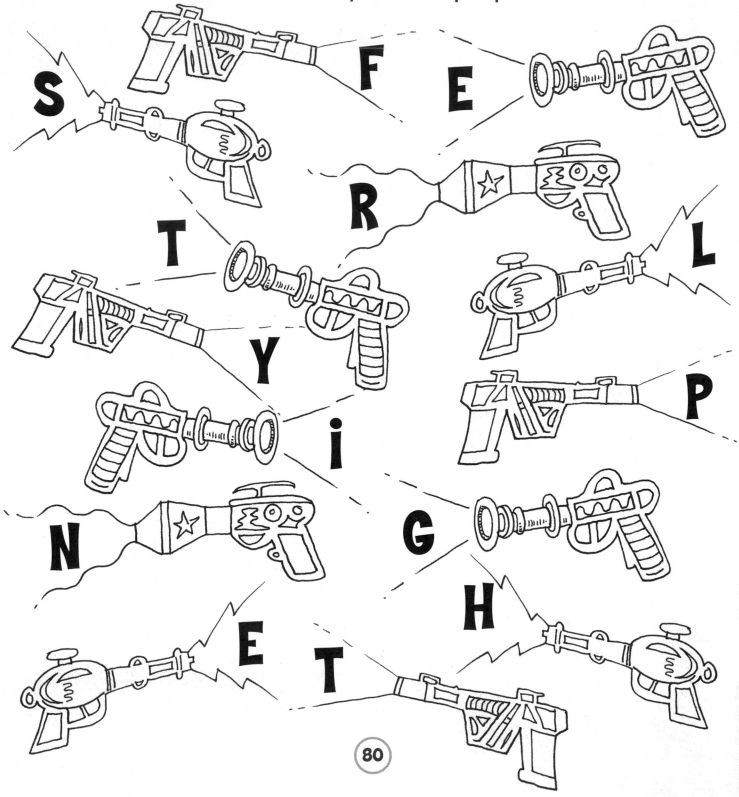

JUST JOKING

Follow the instructions to find the answer to the joke.

Why are cats good at video games?

so	when	because	they
kick	squeak	should	always
save	have	with	back
twenty	stick	nine	lick
clock	lives	paws	whiskers

1. Get rid of words that begin with S.
2. Cross out any word with W in it.
3. Don't use words ending in K.

CIAO ITALIA!

Julia is visiting Italy to see the famous sights. Work out which letters are missing from the alphabet at each landmark to find out which cities she goes to.

BCDEFGHJKLMN OQRTUVWXYZ

ABCDFGHIJKLNP QSTUVWXYZ

BCDEFGHJKOPQ RSTUVWXYZ

BCDFGHIJKMOQ RTUVWXYZ

POWWOW, NOW!

A powwow gives Native Americans the chance to dance and celebrate in a traditional way. Look at the main picture and see which of the shadows matches it, as night begins to fall.

DREAM TEAM

Design a kit for your top team. Base it on their real one,
or make up one of your own.

84

EAGLE EYES

See if you can find the smaller squares somewhere in the main picture.
Write the grid reference for each one.

BETTER, FASTER, HIGHER

Which of these superheroes can fly the highest? Add up the numbers for each one to find out. The biggest total wins!

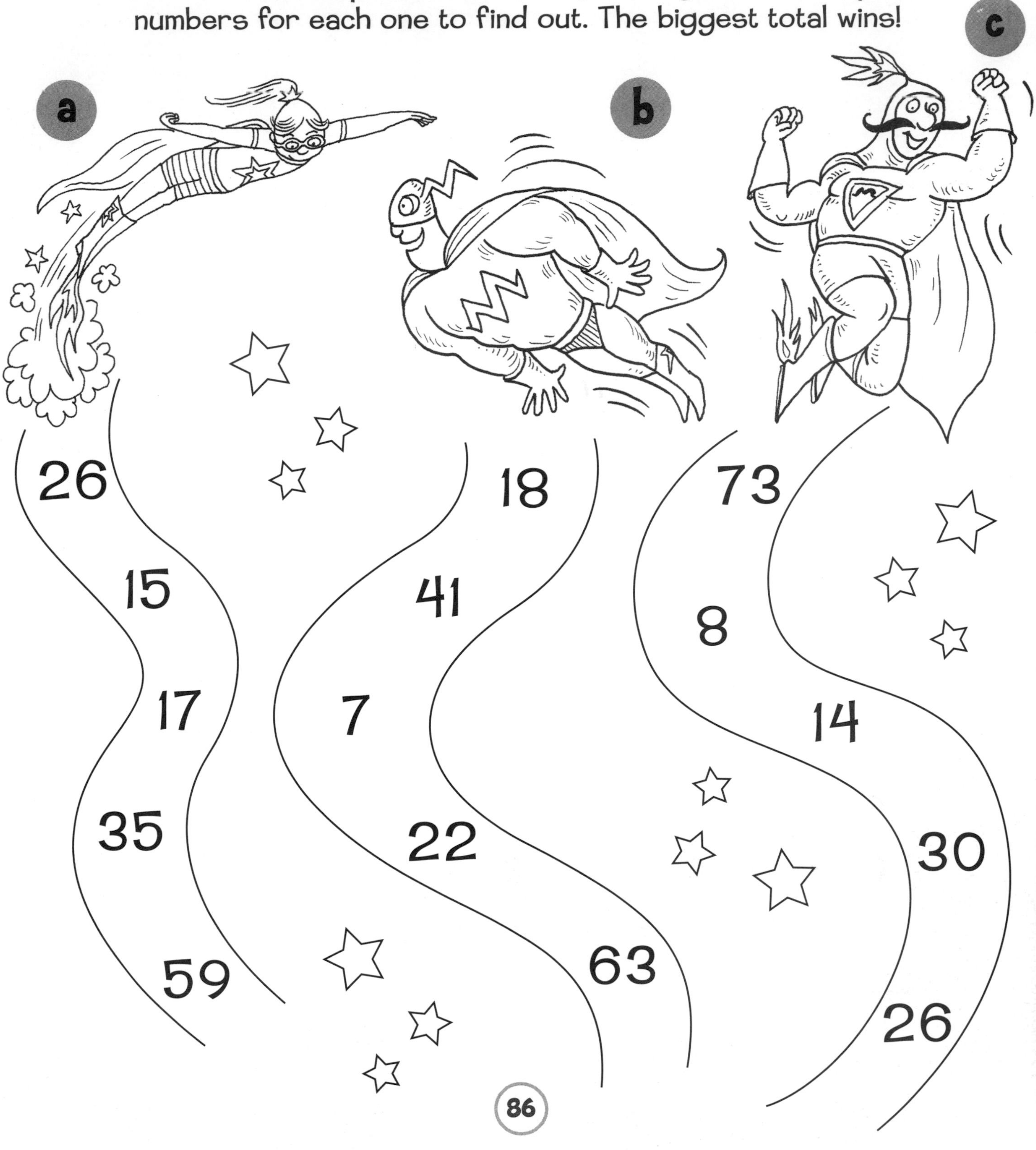

a

b

c

26

15

17

35

59

18

41

7

22

63

73

8

14

30

26

86

IT'S A MYSTERY

There are 20 pets hidden in this wordsearch grid, but no clues to help you find them! Look for them up and down, across and diagonally.

F	T	i	B	B	A	R	R	A	T	F	S
G	O	L	D	F	i	S	H	S	P	D	N
U	E	H	R	T	T	G	L	N	R	T	A
i	D	R	A	P	O	E	i	A	C	E	i
N	U	C	B	M	R	R	Z	K	H	R	L
E	K	H	B	i	S	i	A	E	i	R	O
A	C	i	G	C	L	T	L	i	Z	A	F
P	N	M	Z	A	G	F	E	R	R	P	E
i	E	O	i	O	L	Y	M	R	Y	i	R
G	K	U	D	i	R	J	i	N	A	N	R
P	C	S	E	A	O	U	O	H	D	F	E
A	i	E	N	D	G	P	A	R	R	O	T
R	H	A	S	T	O	R	T	O	i	S	E
R	C	H	i	N	C	H	i	L	L	A	D

FUN IN THE SUN

Work out which clue describes each item and write the number in the right square. All of the rows, columns and diagonals should add up to 15.

1. Fashion for your face
2. Flying high
3. A juicy treat
4. Digging it!
5. Pretty but fragile

6. Yum in the sun!
7. Goes with 4
8. Speedy swimmers
9. A little nipper

PICK A POLE

Which of these totem poles is the odd one out?

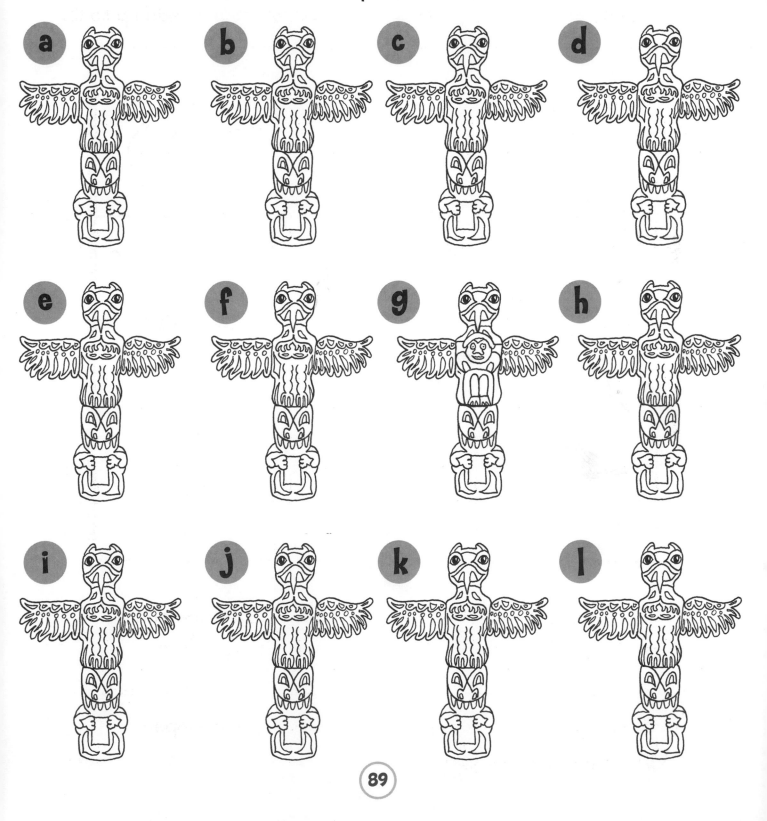

BOWLED OVER

Add up the scores on the pins to find out the total score.

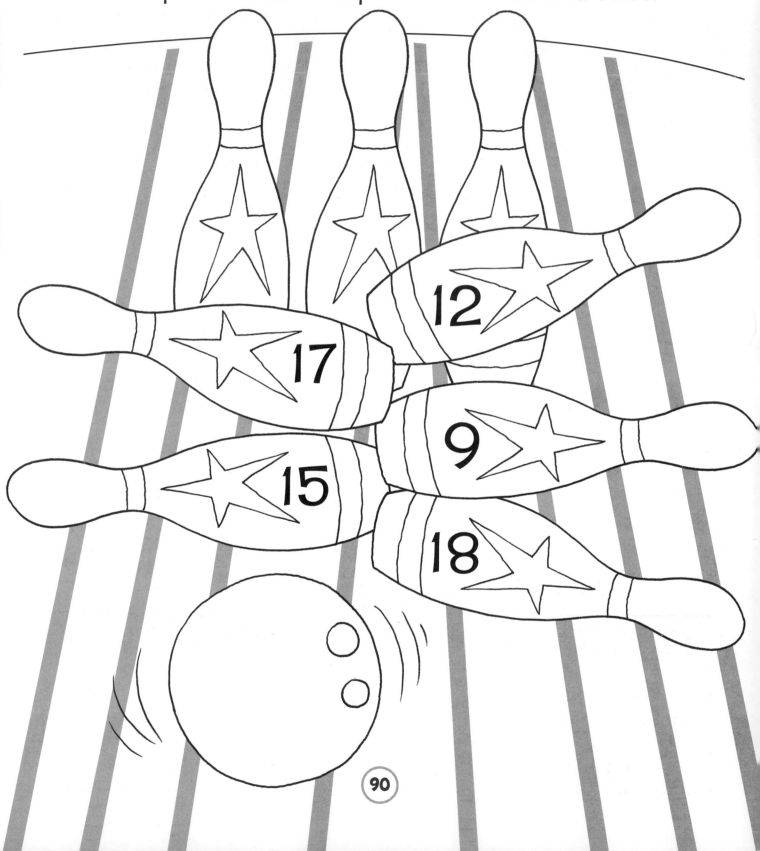

TIME TO EAT!

Use the letters on the clock face to work out which zoo animals are expecting their food at the times shown. Follow the instructions in the box.

> Write down the letters shown by the minute hand, then by the hour hand, for each time. The letters will spell an animal's name. For example, quarter to five = LION.

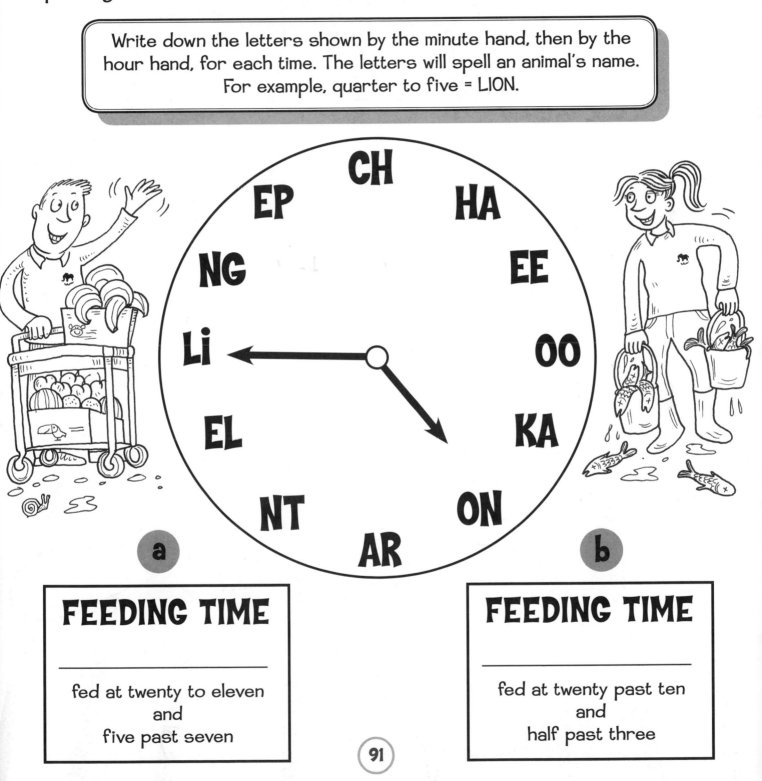

FEEDING TIME

fed at twenty to eleven
and
five past seven

FEEDING TIME

fed at twenty past ten
and
half past three

X-RAY VISION

Imagine you are a superhero with X-ray eyes. That's right, you can see right through things! What is this bad guy carrying in his bag?

MUCKING OUT

Ferdy loves her pony so much, she doesn't even mind mucking out!
Can you find 10 carrots hidden in and around the stables?

ON THE CASE

Helen has forgotten the code to open her suitcase. Can you help her to work it out?

1. Days in May minus days in June
2. Legs on a flamingo times number of blind mice
3. Hours in a day divided by half a dozen
4. Legs on a spider minus Goldilocks' bears

THE OLD WEST

Cross out any letter that appears more than once. The letters that are left will spell the name of a true cowboy state of the USA.

ON YOUR BIKE

Circle every third letter on the mountain bike track to discover
a type of cycling, sometimes known as XC.

BIRD BRAINS

Find all twenty five feathered friends in this giant word search grid.

E	A	L	B	A	T	R	O	S	S	E	P	C	P
H	M	W	O	O	D	W	T	O	U	C	H	T	i
W	E	U	C	U	L	C	K	O	O	A	E	H	G
E	R	R	H	O	R	N	B	i	L	L	A	R	E
A	P	E	N	G	U	i	N	P	W	B	S	U	O
G	E	N	N	G	R	E	B	E	E	i	A	S	N
L	K	i	O	B	P	E	L	i	C	A	N	H	i
E	O	S	T	R	i	C	H	P	E	D	T	T	B
W	O	O	D	P	E	C	K	E	R	H	O	U	O
O	K	R	O	B	D	H	R	T	S	O	U	V	R
R	C	D	T	U	R	K	E	Y	B	R	C	W	E
C	U	U	C	P	A	R	R	O	T	N	A	R	E
A	C	K	A	L	B	F	L	A	M	i	N	G	O

TOUCAN   EAGLE   PENGUIN   CUCKOO
HORNBILL   EMU   FLAMINGO   WREN
OSTRICH   DUCK   PELICAN   ROBIN
KIWI   PHEASANT   PIGEON   CROW
WOODPECKER   ALBATROSS   DOVE   THRUSH
HERON   GREBE   PARROT   TURKEY
OWL

JEWEL THIEF

Which adversary does the Blue Comet find himself up against this time? Use the code key to find out.

DOG TIRED

This pet pup has worn itself out! Look carefully on its bed to find one shape that is different from all the rest.

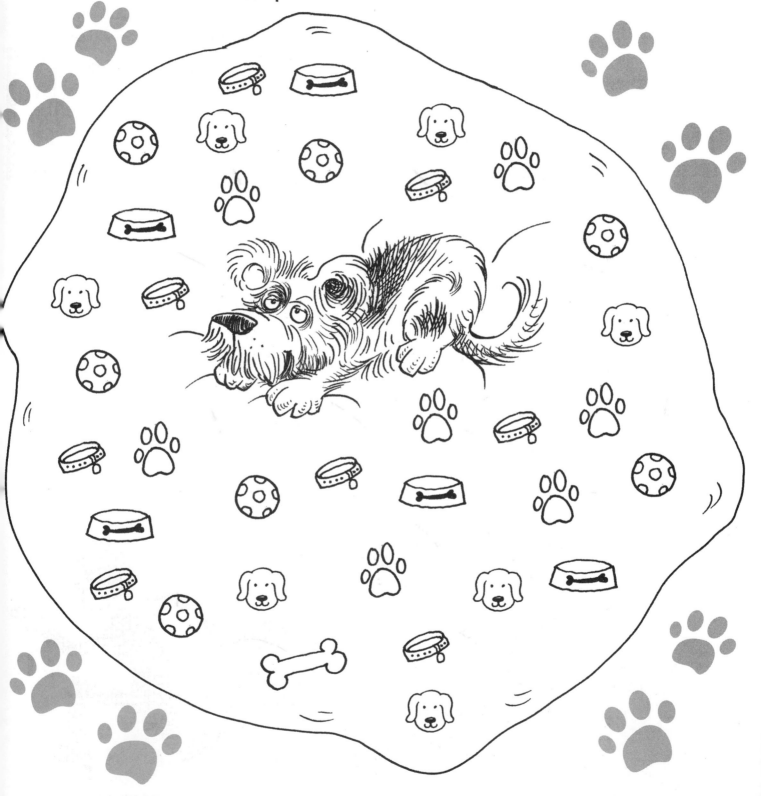

YOU'RE IN CHARGE

Imagine you're the ruler of your own country. What would your flag, money and stamps look like?

HOME, SWEET HOME

Find each of the pieces in the main picture below, and write down the correct grid reference for each.

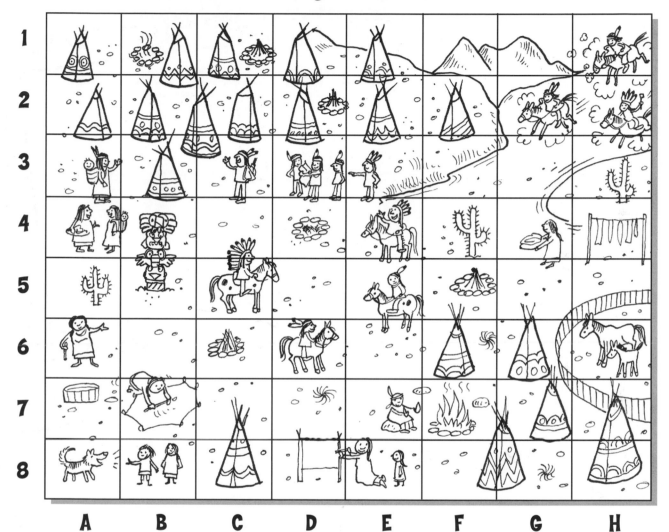

	A	B	C	D	E	F	G	H

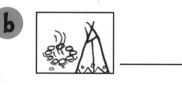

(a) _____

(b) _____

(c) _____

(d) _____

(e) _____

(f) _____

ALL THE BALLS

The mini-grid appears only once in the whole of the larger grid. Can you find it?

ROLL UP, ROLL UP!

How many armadillos are there on this page? Some of them have rolled up in a ball to hide, but you should still count them!

UNDERWATER RESCUE

When things go wrong in the water, you need Aquatar! Which two of these superhero pictures are the same?

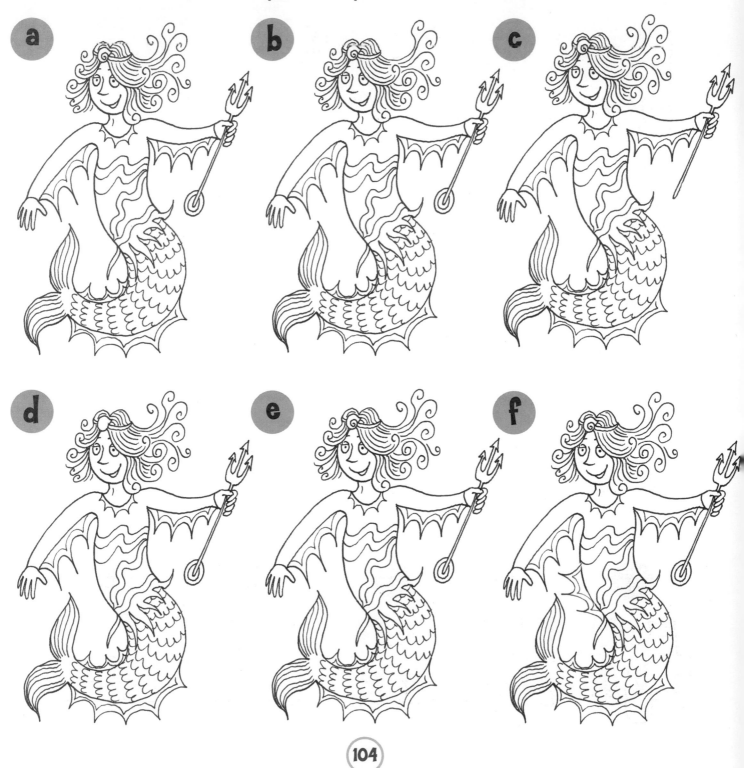

FUNNY BUNNIES

Which of the jigsaw pieces finishes the picture of the
cutest bunnies you could wish to see?

DREAM TICKET

Use the grid references to write down the correct letters. They will spell out the place where the Martinez family are going this summer.

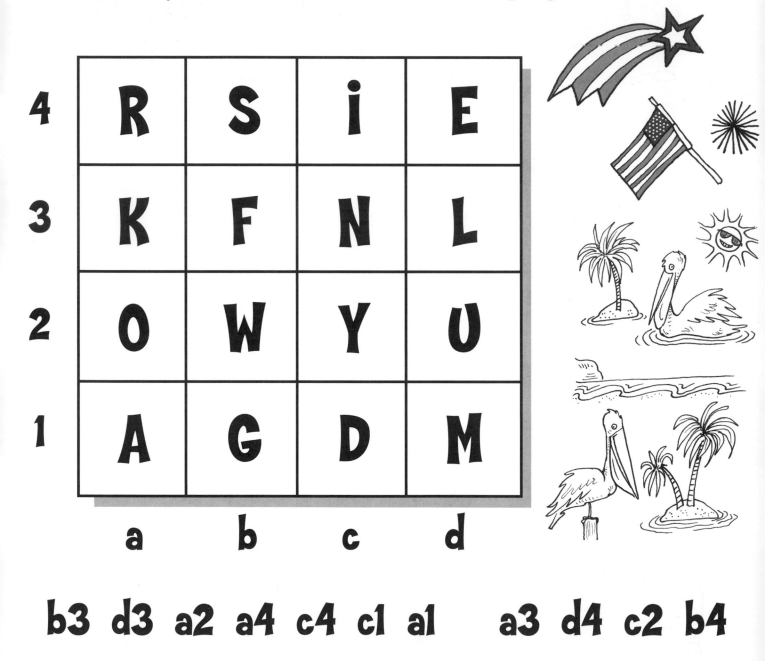

	a	b	c	d
4	R	S	i	E
3	K	F	N	L
2	O	W	Y	U
1	A	G	D	M

b3 d3 a2 a4 c4 c1 a1   a3 d4 c2 b4

_ _ _ _ _ _ _   _ _ _ _

SADDLE UP

Help the cowgirl find her way through the desert and ride into town for the rodeo.

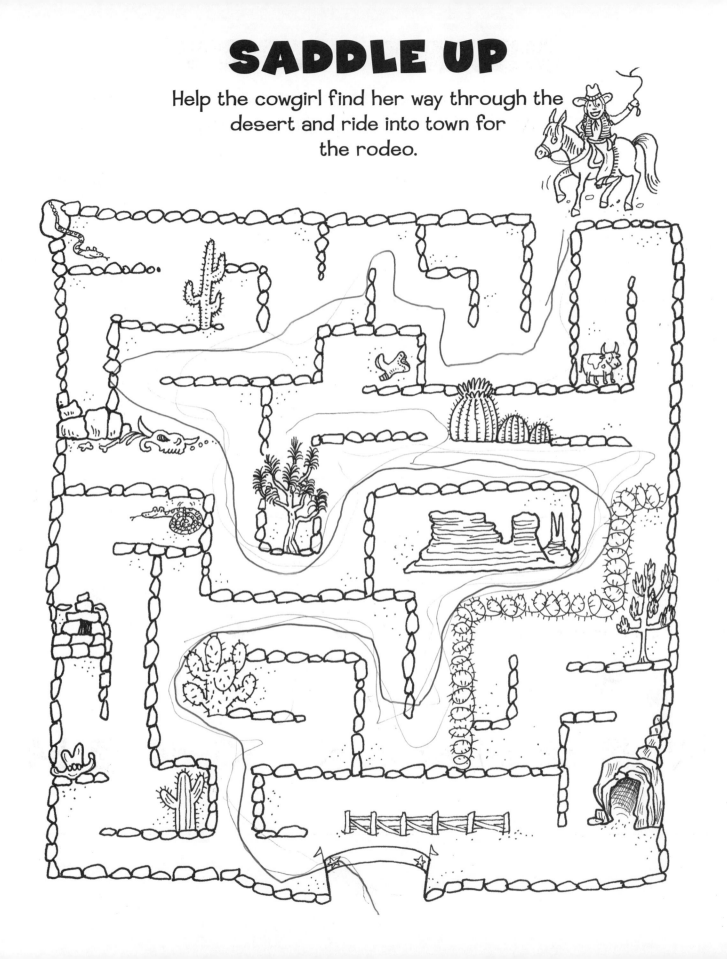

GOING FOR GOLD

Cross out all of the letters that appear twice. The remaining letters will spell a sporting superstar!

J U E S
C A I N E
R
R D R T L
K O C K
J B D

_ _ _ _ _ _ _ _ _

HILARIOUS HYBRID

What do you think it would look like if you crossed a lion with a rhino? Or an ostrich with a penguin? Draw your silliest idea here and give it a name.

ROLL UP!

COME AND SEE THE INCREDIBLE _____ !

BOO! HISS!

The evil Doc Paradox has cloned himself, but one of the clones has gone slightly wrong. Which one is different from all the rest?

CUDDLY CREATURES

Study the map of the urban zoo and use it to answer the questions.

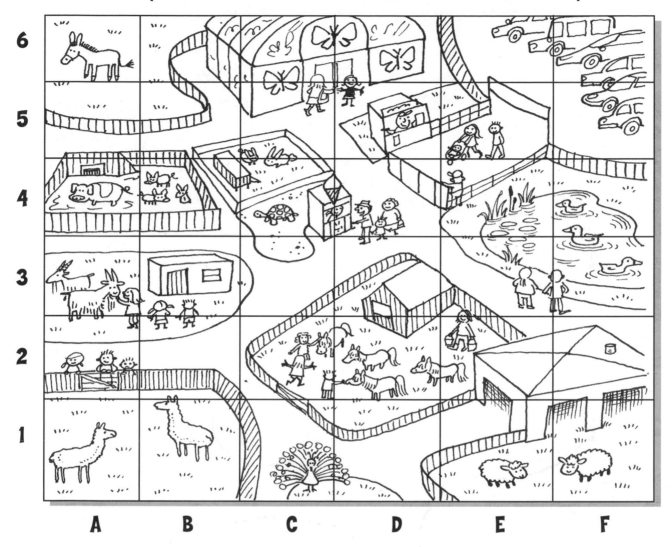

1. Which bird is roaming free in C1?

_____

2. In which square can you stroke the goats?

_____

3. Where should you go to see the tortoise?

_____

4. Where is the entrance gate?

_____

5. What are the babies called in B4?

_____

6. What animal can you feed from the gate in A2?

_____

GET PACKING

Help Luisa find 10 items that go together to make 5 pairs. The other things are staying behind!

THE LONE RANGER

Can you find the word RANGER hidden just once in this grid?
Look across, up and down, and diagonally.

R	A	N	G	G	E	R	E	E	G
A	R	E	G	A	N	A	N	R	A
N	A	N	G	R	A	N	A	A	G
E	N	A	E	N	E	N	G	N	R
R	A	R	R	G	A	E	A	R	E
A	A	E	A	E	G	R	A	N	G
R	E	G	A	N	G	R	A	N	R
E	G	N	E	E	G	A	E	G	E
R	A	G	E	R	N	E	N	E	E
G	R	E	G	A	N	A	R	G	N

113

SPORTS SQUARE

Work out which clue describes each item and write the number in the right square. All of the rows, columns and diagonals should add up to 15.

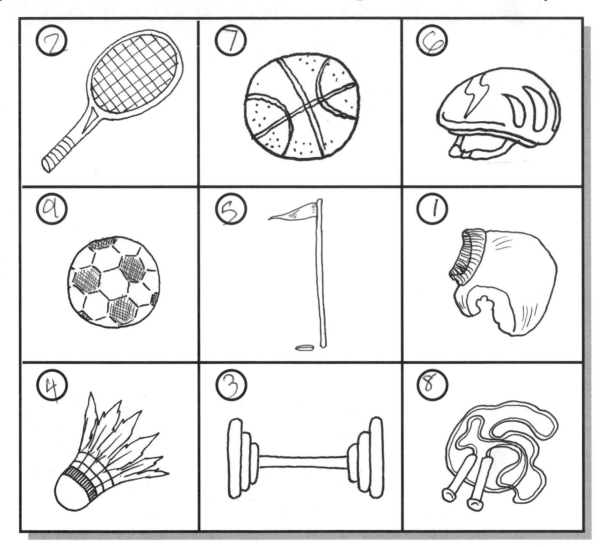

1. You wanna fight?
2. A sport with aces
3. Heavy, man!
4. Light as a feather
5. A hole in one?

6. Head case!
7. Slam dunk
8. Give it a twirl
9. Back of the net!

LION LAUGHS

Follow the instructions to find the answer to the joke.

What did the lion say when it ate the clown?

because	~~growl~~	~~but~~	huge
~~his~~	~~brought~~	~~did~~	~~long~~
~~not~~	he	~~she~~	~~was~~
~~back~~	~~great~~	tasted	~~breath~~
funny	~~wrong~~	~~strange~~	~~again~~

1. Get rid of words with three letters. ✓
2. Cross out words containing G.
3. Lose any words that start with B.

TO THE RESCUE!

Omegaman and his sidekick Delta have swung in to this party to save the day! How many hidden party hooters can you find?

PERFECT PET

If you were allowed any pet in the world, what would you choose?

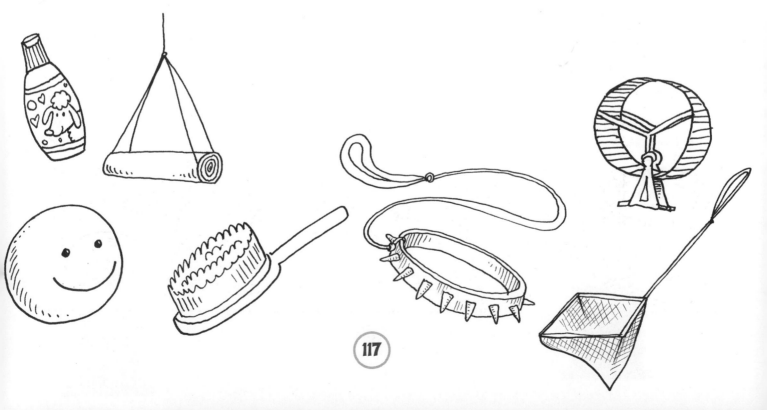

LADY LIBERTY

Welcome to the USA! Study the famous Statue of Liberty and then see which of the silhouettes is an exact match.

THE SILVER SADDLE

Welcome to the Silver Saddle Saloon! See if you can find the smaller squares somewhere in the main picture. Write the grid reference for each one.

COACH GOODWAY

What sport does Coach Goodway teach?
Use the clues to work it out.

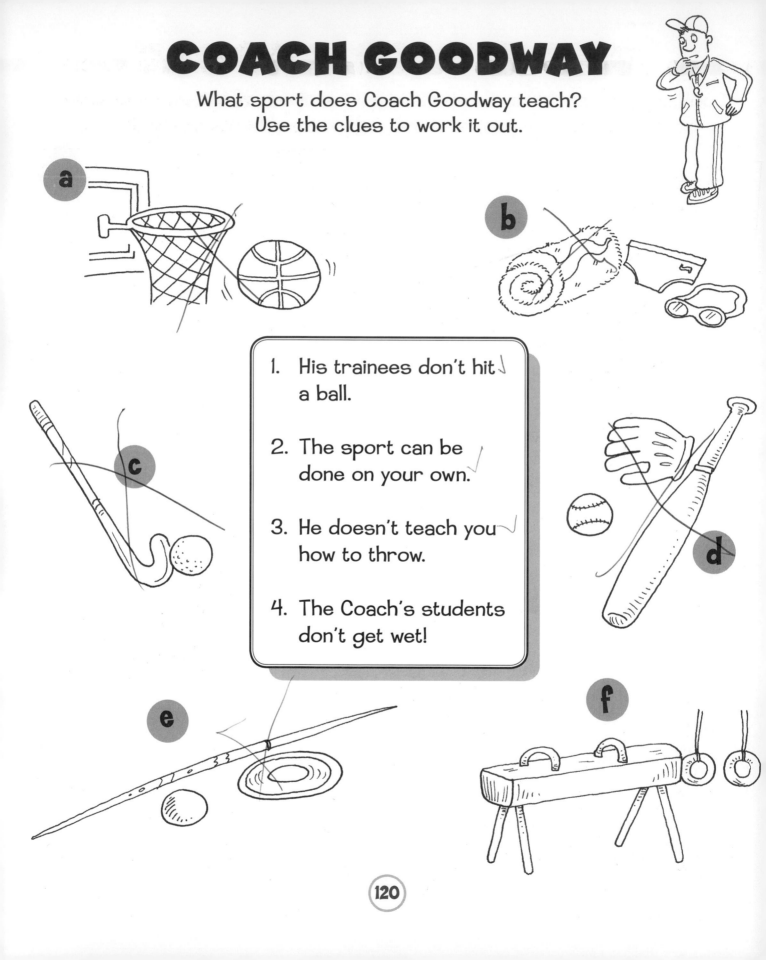

1. His trainees don't hit a ball.

2. The sport can be done on your own.

3. He doesn't teach you how to throw.

4. The Coach's students don't get wet!

TALL AND SMALL

Look carefully at the mixed up picture. Draw each of the squares in the correct place on the grid to put the picture back together again.

HELP ME!

Captain Schnurrbart to the rescue!
Look carefully to find six differences
between these two scenes.

BIRD TALK

Cross out every other letter, starting with T and moving clockwise, to find out where this chatty pet would live in the wild.

SNORKEL SCARE

Put these pictures in the correct order to tell the story properly.

ON THE LOOKOUT

There's a new bad guy in town! Finish this Wild West wanted poster with your own cowboy criminal.

WANTED
Dead or alive

REWARD OF
$250,000

WIN OR LOSE?

Shade in all the squares containing F, L and O. The remaining letters will spell the answer to the joke.

Why didn't the artist ever win at sports?

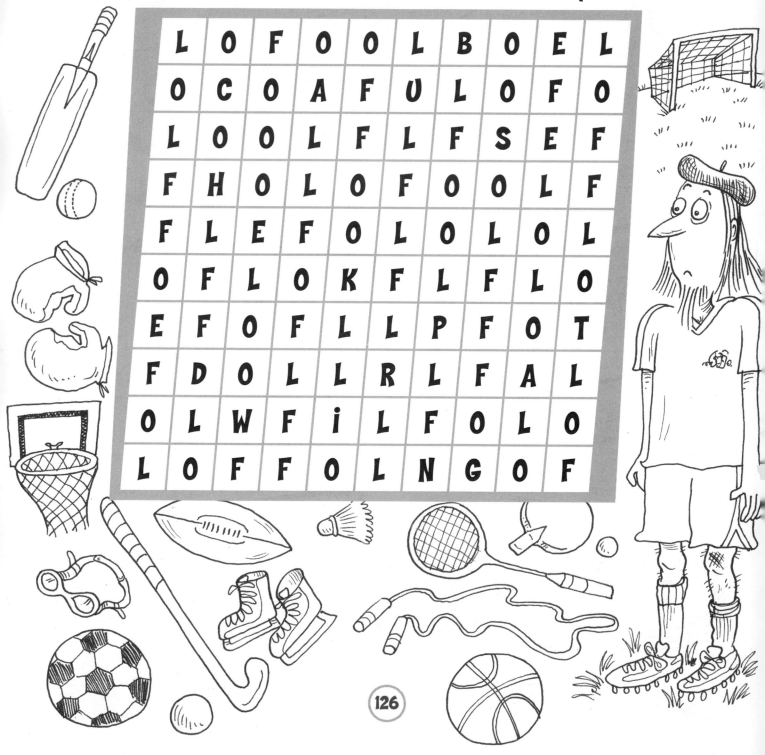

L	O	F	O	O	L	B	O	E	L
O	C	O	A	F	U	L	O	F	O
L	O	O	L	F	L	F	S	E	F
F	H	O	L	O	F	O	O	L	F
F	L	E	F	O	L	O	L	O	L
O	F	L	O	K	F	L	F	L	O
E	F	O	F	L	L	P	F	O	T
F	D	O	L	L	R	L	F	A	L
O	L	W	F	i	L	F	O	L	O
L	O	F	F	O	L	N	G	O	F

ICE, ICE BABY

Solve the sums and find a path across the ice
stepping only on answers that are odd numbers.

6 x 8

53 - 21

45 ÷ 5

7 x 3

24 + 54

66 - 34

16 + 19

56 ÷ 8

38 + 38

64 ÷ 8

96 - 27

7 x 6

4 x 12

11 x 3

SUPERFOODS

Use the grid references to write down the correct letters.
They will spell out Captain Cobalt's top choice on a menu.

	a	b	c	d
4	A	P	E	H
3	U	N	Y	F
2	R	E	S	B
1	M	L	C	i

d2 b1 a3 b2 d2 c4 a2 a2 c3   b4 d1 c4

___ ___ ___ ___ ___ ___ ___ ___ ___   ___ ___ ___

IT'S A STICK UP

How many stick insects are hiding here?

MAKING CAMP

Use the clues to work out what each of the girls is camping in, and where they are going.

	Tent	Camper van	Tepee
Amy			
Leigh			
Millie			

Amy isn't going to Italy.

Millie's home has wheels.

The girl in the tent is going to Spain.

Leigh and Millie aren't going to France.

	France	Italy	Spain
Amy			
Leigh			
Millie			

OUTLAWED

Billy the Kid has escaped from jail! Follow the directions to find out where he's hiding.

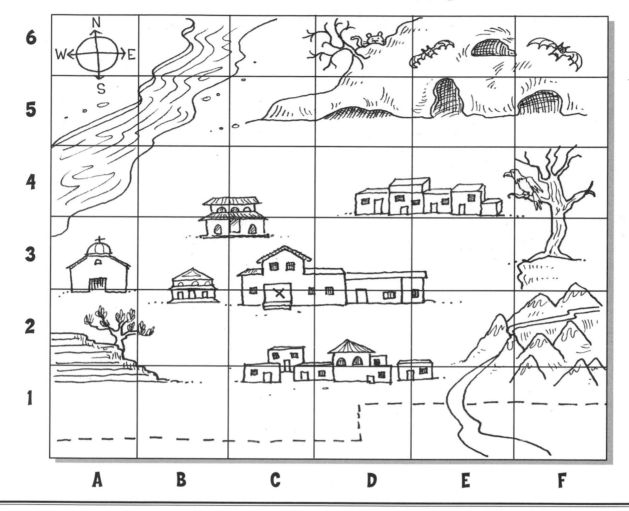

1. After leaving jail, in C3, he headed 1 square south for the border, but went 2 squares east to avoid the huts.

2. At the mountains he cut south again for 1 square, crossed the border, and ran 3 squares west.

3. He sneaked 4 squares north, past Lone Pine Ridge and the church.

4. At the Rio Grande river he headed east 1 square, then north 1 square, then east 1 square again. Where should the sheriff look for him?

THE WINNER IS...

You decide! Draw the race winners on the podium.
They can be competitors in any sport you like.

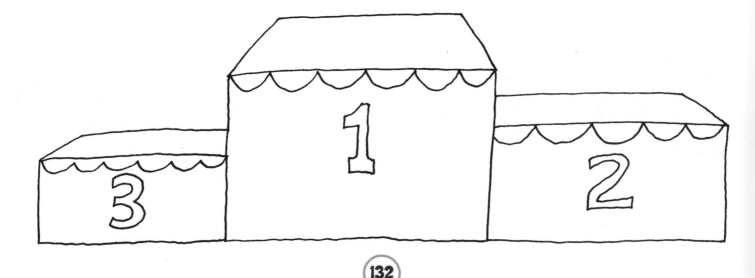

ANIMAL MUDDLE!

What on earth is a ferkey? Or a waltle? Hang on a minute, these animal names are all mixed up! Split them up and put them back together properly to spell six real animals.

FER KEY

MON SEL

WAL TLE

TUR VER

WEA RUS

BEA RET

STRANDED

Daisy Dolittle is stranded on top of the maze tower in Dubai! Only Spiderguy can help! Find a way up the building to rescue Daisy, and then back down the other side.

PUT IN THEIR PLACE

Put the pets in the sudoku grid so that each row, column
and mini-grid has only one of each type.

CITY SEARCH

Where is Vicky going for her special trip? Look along each row to find one letter that appears in every city name. Find all six letters to spell her vacation destination.

Versailles	Avignon	Vienna	Vilnius	___
San Diego	Seville	Zagreb	Rome	___
Milan	Montreal	Dublin	Sydney	___
Lima	Sofia	Paris	Kingston	___
Cardiff	Valencia	Calais	Moscow	___
New York	Canberra	Prague	Seoul	___

CATCHING CATTLE

These cattle have been branded to show who owns them.
Match each one to its owner by solving the sums.

$24 \div 6 =$

4

7

9

$72 \div 8 =$

6

5

8

$45 \div 9 =$

$48 \div 6 =$

$54 \div 9 =$

$49 \div 7 =$

SPORTS SEARCH

Look carefully in the grid to find fifteen sports that don't hit the headlines all the time. They can be hidden across, up and down, and diagonally.

POLO   **NETBALL**   **JUDO**

FENCING   **SOFTBALL**   **KARATE**

LACROSSE   **SURFING**   **SNOOKER**

DIVING   **BOULES**   **DRESSAGE**

SQUASH   **CLIMBING**   **HURLING**

S	K	A	R	N	S	U	R	F	I	N	G
U	G	S	D	R	E	S	S	A	G	E	i
R	N	N	J	U	D	T	N	E	T	S	N
H	i	O	L	P	N	S	B	A	B	U	G
U	C	O	A	S	O	Q	R	A	C	R	N
R	N	K	C	S	O	A	A	J	L	L	i
L	E	E	R	E	K	S	J	U	L	L	B
i	F	R	O	R	E	H	V	D	i	A	M
N	E	T	S	D	i	V	i	N	G	B	i
G	J	H	S	A	U	Q	S	V	i	T	L
S	Q	U	E	P	B	O	U	L	D	F	C
J	U	D	D	R	E	S	S	O	L	O	P
P	O	L	B	O	U	L	E	S	Q	S	Q

CREATURE COUNT

Study this picture of the rainforest canopy and see how many of each creature you can count.

Butterflies =

Snakes =

Beetles =

Birds =

FALLING OR FLYING?

SuperPete is holding on to something - but is he flying, or hitching a lift?
You decide, and draw what's high in the sky with him.

GO, GINNY, GO!

Help Ginny the guinea pig find her way to her friends by following the arrows in the right direction each time.

START

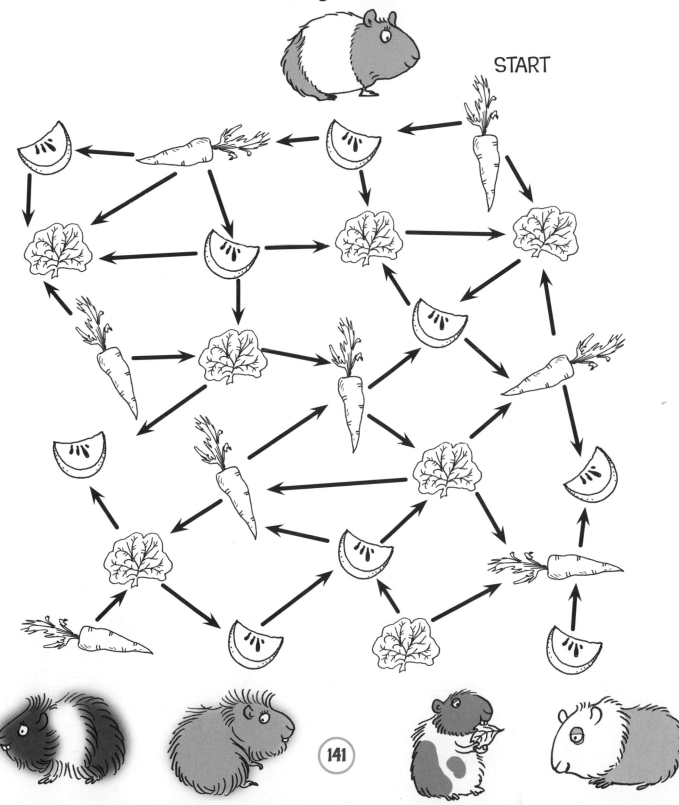

OFF WE GO!

Unscramble the letters on each luggage label to find out which cities everyone is going on their travels.

ULCKADAN

New Zealand

EASTHN

Greece

NTOOTOR

Canada

DNSYEY

Australia

NGKBAOK

Thailand

IRCAO

Egypt

142

BIRD'S EYE VIEW

Study the shootout picture, and then decide which of the smaller pictures is the proper bird's eye view of the scene.

a

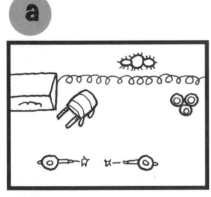

b

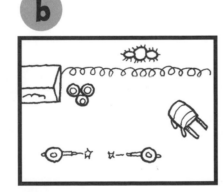

c

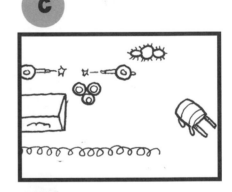

d

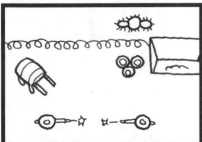

e

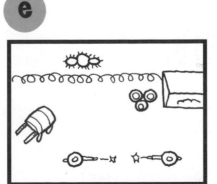

f

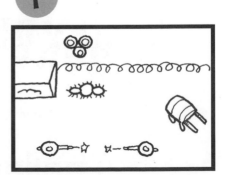

SPORTS CAMP

Find out what camp activities are scheduled at the times shown, using the unusual clock. Follow the instructions carefully.

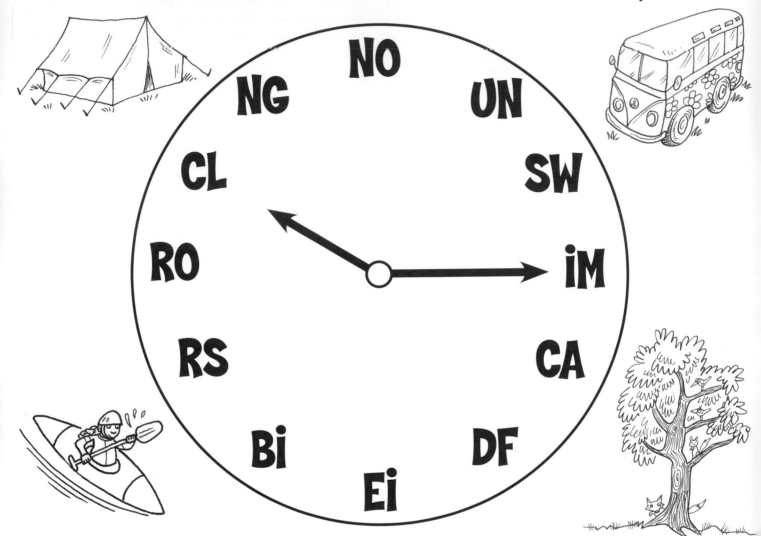

Write down the letters shown by the minute hand, then by the hour hand, for each time. Together, they will spell the activities you are looking for. For example, ten past three = SWIM.

a ten to three
twenty five to eleven

b twenty past twelve
half past eleven

FOOTPRINTS

The mini-grid appears only once in the whole of the larger grid.
Can you find it?

LASER LINES

Fill in the blanks using the letters RAYGUN, in any order, so that every row, column and mini-grid contains each letter only once.

STABLE SHADOWS

Look carefully at the picture of Belinda with her pony.
Which of the silhouettes matches it exactly?

CITY SCAPE

Finish the buildings and add your own designs
to make a city you would love to explore.

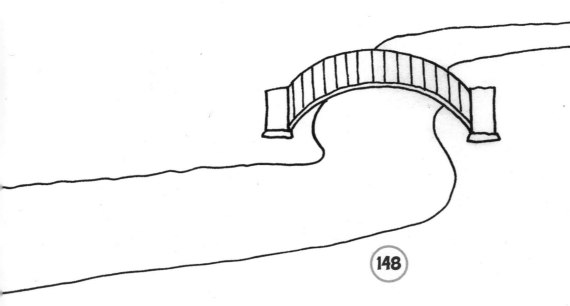

YEE HA!

Which two of these cowboys are exactly the same?

MUSCLE MAN

Use the grid references to write down the correct letters. They will spell out what sport this muscle man competes in.

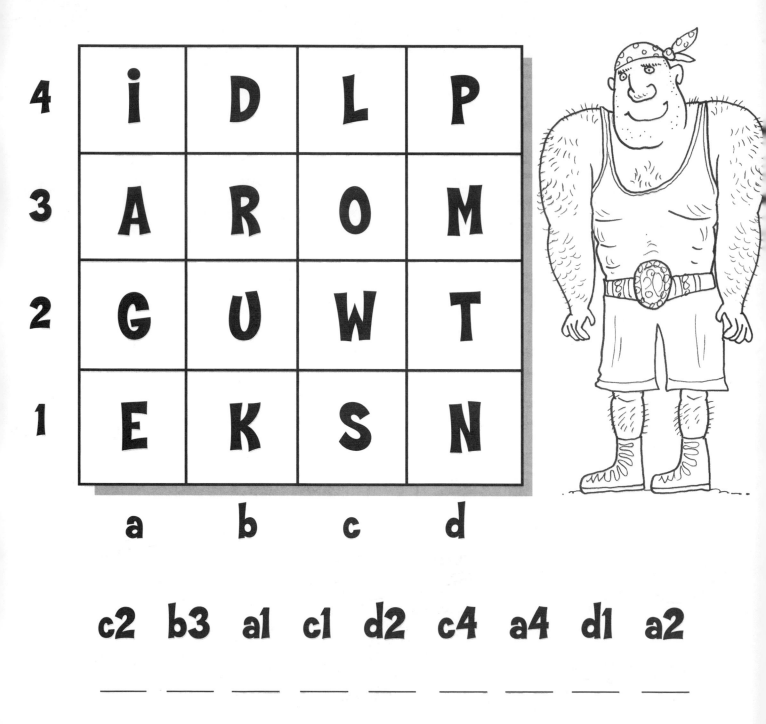

	a	b	c	d
4	i	D	L	P
3	A	R	O	M
2	G	U	W	T
1	E	K	S	N

c2   b3   a1   c1   d2   c4   a4   d1   a2

___ ___ ___ ___ ___ ___ ___ ___ ___

A PRICKLY SITUATION

Can you find a way through this porcupine's prickly quill maze?

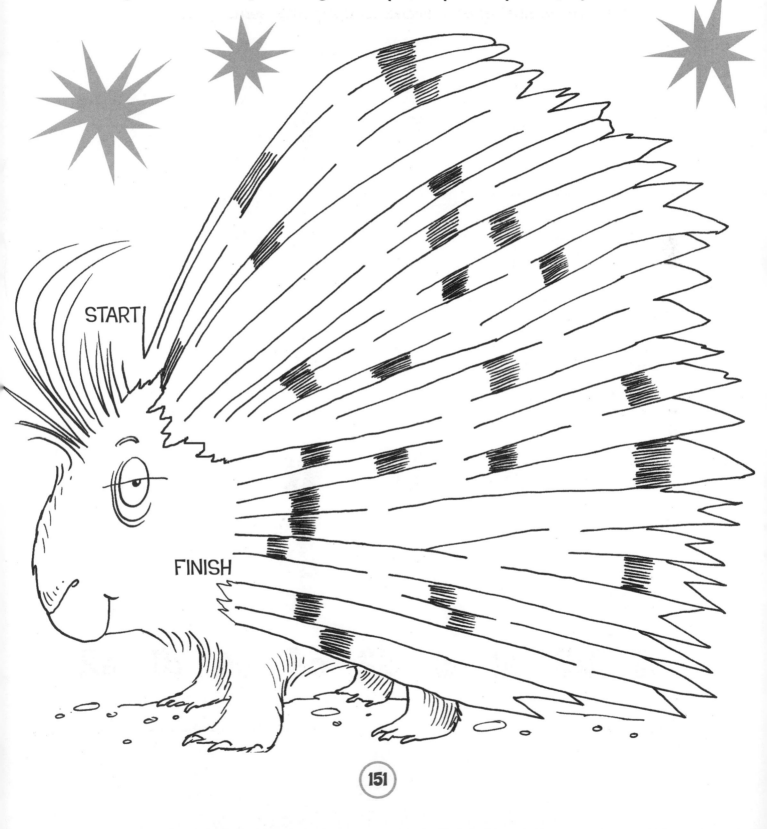

START

FINISH

A BUSY DAY

Help Captain Flash rescue everyone! You must pass through each circle only once, and aren't allowed along the same path twice.

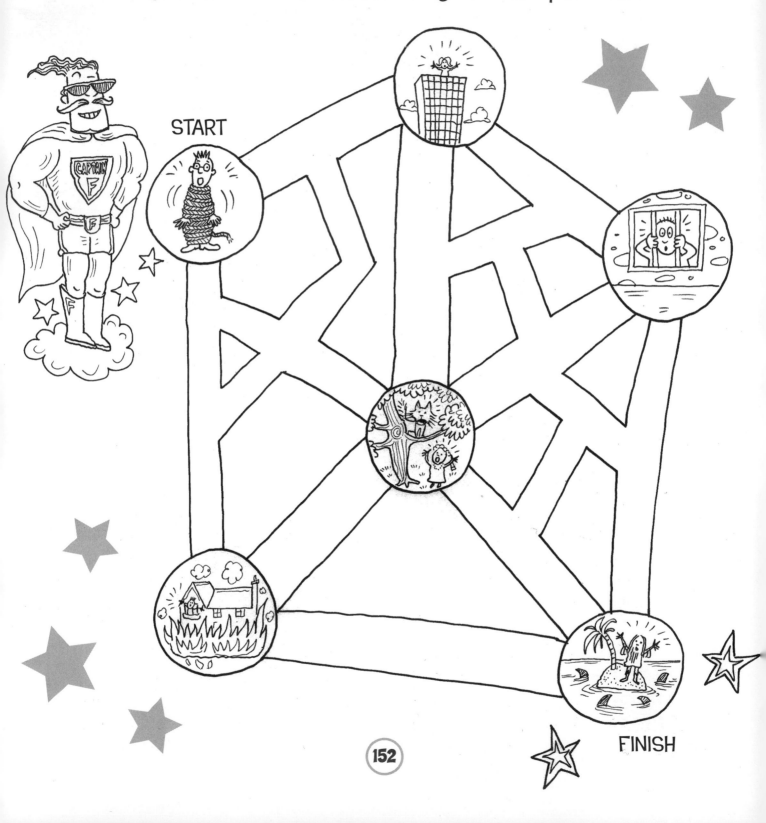

START

FINISH

PETS ON PARADE

Which pet should replace the question mark to complete the pattern properly?

a

b

c

d

153

ROAD TRIP

Are we nearly there yet?! Kill time by making new words with three or more letters from the letters below. One has been done to get you started.

THIS iS BORING!

1. GHOST
2. _____
3. _____
4. _____
5. _____
6. _____
7. _____
8. _____
9. _____
10. _____

11. _____
12. _____
13. _____
14. _____
15. _____
16. _____
17. _____
18. _____
19. _____
20. _____

THE ACCUSED

See if you can find the smaller squares somewhere in the main picture.
Write the grid reference for each one.

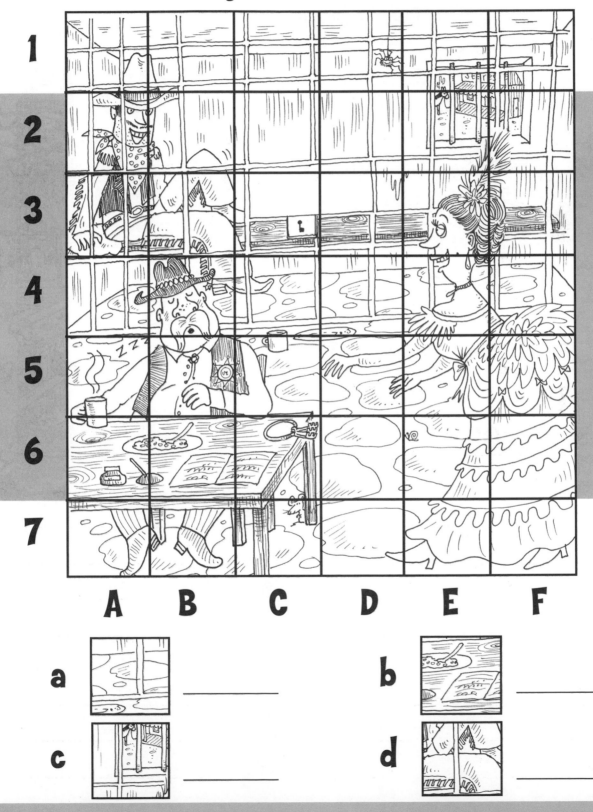

a _____

b _____

c _____

d _____

MAKING A SPLASH

Everyone here is getting fabulously fit! Look carefully to find three extra people in the bottom picture.

NIGHT VISION

What kind of animal is peering at you from this page? Finish it yourself - make it cute, fierce, or totally freaky!

CHEMICAL CHAOS

If A = 1, B = 2, C=3 and so on, work out what each of evil Doc Paradox's formulas is called.

2.18.1.9.14

2.12.1.19.20.5.18

4.9.19.1.16.16.5.1.18.9.15

13.5.7.1.2.5.12.3.8

10.21.9.3.5

ON THE PROWL

Look carefully at the mixed up picture. Draw each of the squares in the correct place on the grid to put the picture back together again.

LIBERTY LAUGHS

Follow the instructions to find the answer to the joke.

Why does the Statue of Liberty stand at the entrance to New York?

really	how	would
shall	wants	should
because	feels	it
twice	can't	too
keeps	think	sit
down	steel	tired

1. Don't keep words with an H in.
2. Cross out words with five letters.
3. Get rid of words containing a double letter.

CAUGHT OUT

Look carefully to find ten differences between the two pictures.

SPORTS SUDOKU

Help Coach Goodway fill in the grid so that each row, column and mini-grid has one of each piece of equipment.

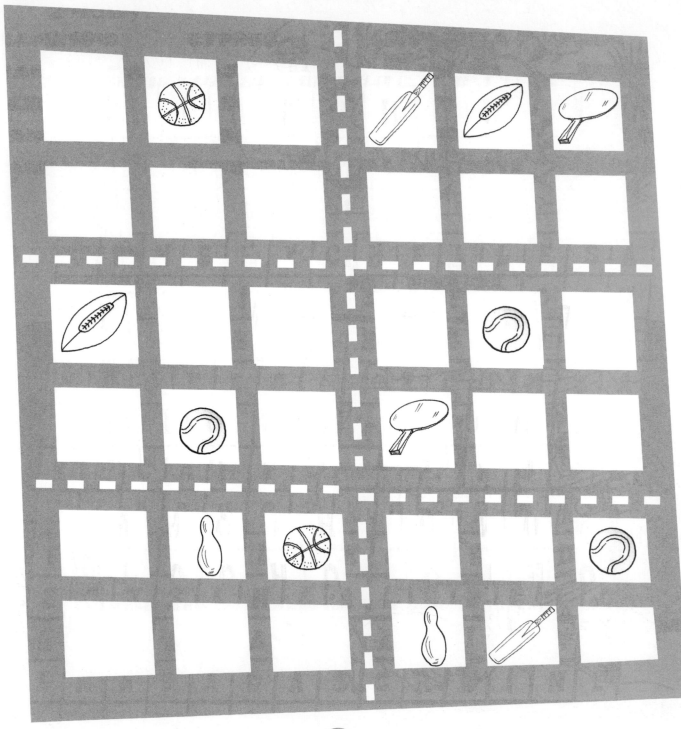

ENDANGERED SPECIES

Can you find the word RHINO hidden only once in the grid?

R	N	O	N	O	R	H	i	i	N
H	i	i	R	H	i	R	O	R	H
N	H	R	H	i	N	i	O	R	H
O	R	H	i	N	O	N	R	H	i
R	H	H	N	R	H	i	R	H	i
H	i	N	N	O	H	R	H	i	N
i	N	O	O	R	H	i	O	R	H
O	N	O	H	N	O	O	N	i	H
N	O	N	O	R	H	i	O	H	R
O	H	N	O	H	O	H	O	O	i

BLAST AWAY!

Which of the pieces finishes the jigsaw properly?

WHO LIVES HERE?

What sort of pet do you think lives in here?

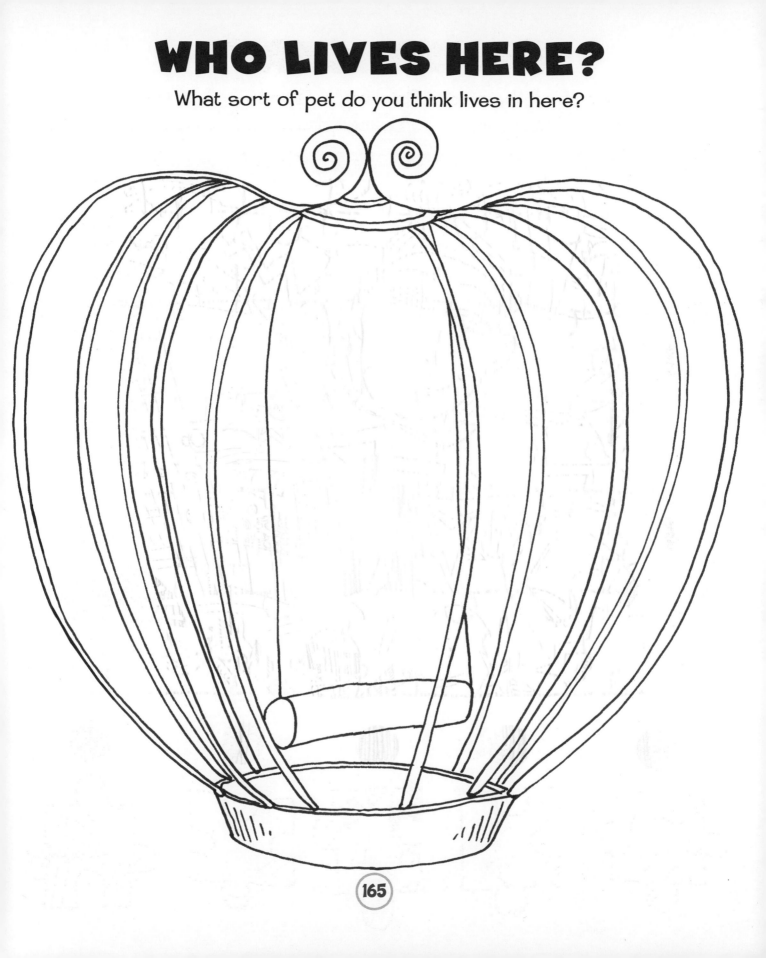

TOP TRIP

Shade in all the squares containing B, L or M to find out what Susie has wished for at her dream destination.

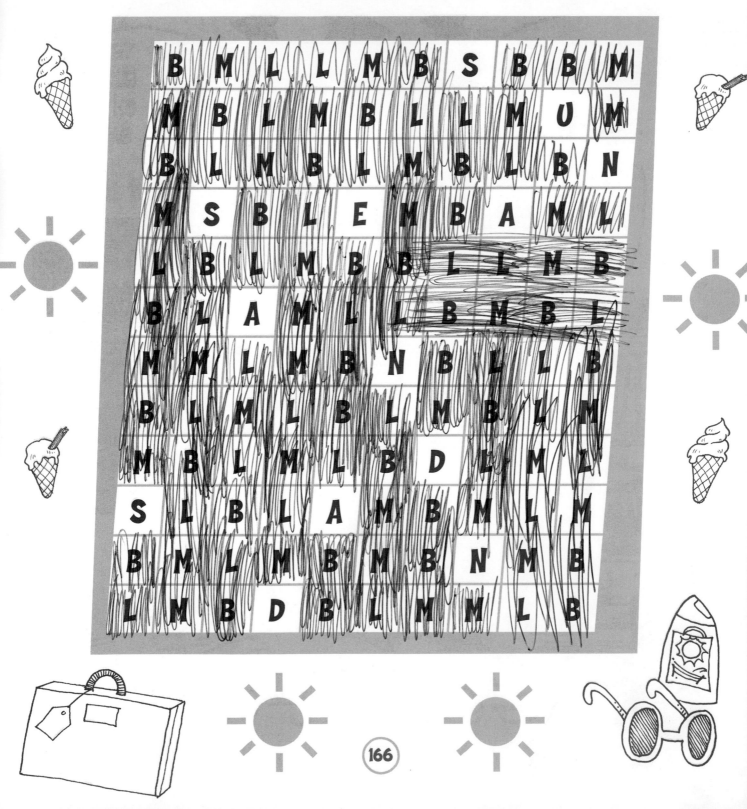

WANTED!

Use the clues to work out which of these cowboys is wanted by the sheriff.

1. He doesn't have a black hat.
2. He isn't wearing a neckerchief.
3. He doesn't have a beard.
4. His hat has a badge on it.

WINTER THRILLS

Find the letters that are missing from the alphabet in each section, and use them to spell the names of four winter sports.

ABDEFHJKMO PQSTVWXYZ

BCDEFHJLMO PQRUVWXYZ

ABCDFHIJKMNO PQRSTVWXYZ

ABCDEFGHLN OQRTVWXYZ

OUT IN AFRICA

Kate and Nate are on safari. Follow the directions to find out which animals they find at the end of their expedition.

1. They drive east 1 square then south to see the giraffes.

2. From B4 they travel three squares east to see the zebras.

3. They head south one square and stop to see the elephants and the meerkats.

4. They continue south for one square, then head southwest. Finally, they travel due west again.

What animals do they find?

PARTY PROTECTOR

See if you can find the smaller squares somewhere in the main picture. Write the grid reference for each one.

A B C D E F G H

 **a** _____

 **b** _____

 **c** _____

 **d** _____

 **e** _____

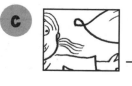 **f** _____

HAMSTER RUN

Help Hatty the hamster through the tubes to the water bottle, passing all five carrots along the way. She can't run along a tube more than once, and must collect each tasty morsel!

IT'S SNOW TIME!

Fortunately for these people, it's snowing on the slopes! The mini-grid appears only once in the whole of the larger grid. Can you find it?

TERRIFIC TENTS!

Decorate this tepee with your best designs.
Use the other ones to inspire you!

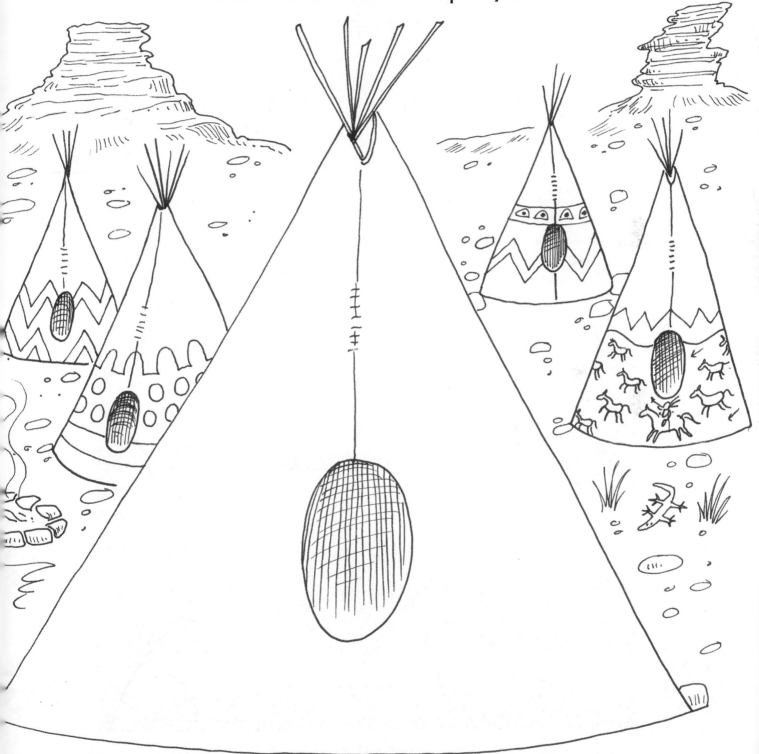

STARTING BLOCKS

Which race are these swimmers about to start?
Use the code key to find out.

IN A FLAP

Cross out the letters that appear twice.
The remaining letters will spell a type of penguin.

_ _ _ _ _ _ _ _

R N F N G P

F H R P O D T

A M B L G

U B A

SUPER STRENGTH

What is this superhero moving to rescue Trinny's dog? You decide!

TANGLED UP

Work your way along the strings to find
a way to the saucer of milk.

ISLAND DREAM

Which of these islands would you like to visit? Find them all in the grid, hidden across, up and down, and diagonally.

MAURITIUS   CYPRUS   SRI LANKA   KOS

MADAGASCAR   MAJORCA   MALDIVES   RHODES

BERMUDA   MENORCA   CORFU   SICILY

JAMAICA   CUBA   TENERIFE   HAWAII

TASMANIA   SEYCHELLES   LANZAROTE   BARBADOS

C	P	M	S	E	Y	C	H	E	L	L	E	S	A
T	Y	E	B	I	I	R	S	U	F	R	O	C	M
E	S	N	A	B	C	Y	R	U	S	K	J	A	L
N	U	O	R	E	O	I	I	R	C	T	M	S	A
E	I	R	B	R	R	Z	L	H	Y	E	A	E	N
R	T	C	A	M	F	U	A	Y	P	N	J	V	Z
I	I	A	D	U	C	Y	N	C	R	E	O	I	A
F	R	H	O	D	E	S	K	U	U	R	R	D	R
E	U	K	S	A	M	E	A	L	S	B	C	L	O
H	A	W	A	T	A	S	M	A	N	I	A	A	T
E	M	A	D	A	G	A	S	C	A	R	I	M	E
H	A	W	A	I	I	A	C	I	A	M	A	J	T

COWBOY TRAIL

Follow in the footsteps of this lonesome cowboy and fill
in the numbers, adding eight each time.

8

16

56

88

CAPSIZED

This boat race isn't going to plan.
What do you think has happened?

RED ALERT

Use the grid references to write down the correct letters. They will spell one of the last two places where orangutans are left in the wild.

	a	b	c	d
4	U	B	Y	L
3	R	I	S	O
2	E	A	N	H
1	T	D	C	M

b4 d3 a3 c2 a2 d3

___ ___ ___ ___ ___ ___

UNMASKED!

How many times can you find the word MASK hidden in the grid?

```
M  A                    M    M  A  S        S
S  K  A  M  A     A  K  S  S  A     M
S  A     M  A  S  K  K  A  K        M
A  K              M  K              A
M  M              M  A              S
K  A  M  A  K  S  A  M  A  S  K
S  A  S  A  A  M  S  M  A  K
K  K  B           A  K  M  S
```

THE
TOTALLY BRILLIANT
SUPER
PUZZLE
BOOK

ANSWERS

3 WALKING THE DOG

4 GREEK ODYSSEY

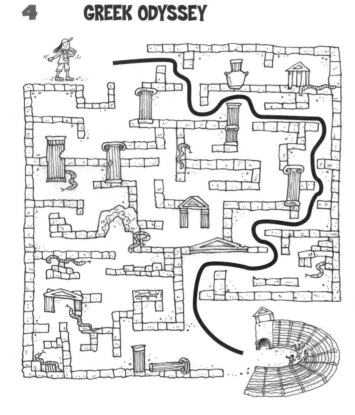

5 COWBOY CRACKER

It was a little hoarse

6 SLALOM SCORE

a = 41

b = 38

8 SIX PACK

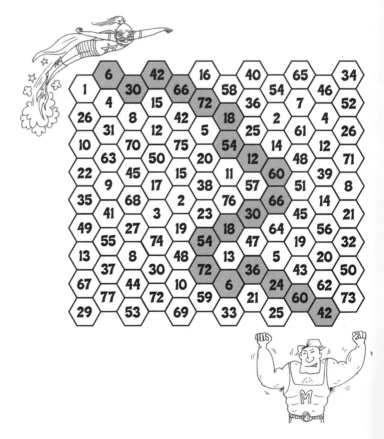

9   MOUSE TRAP

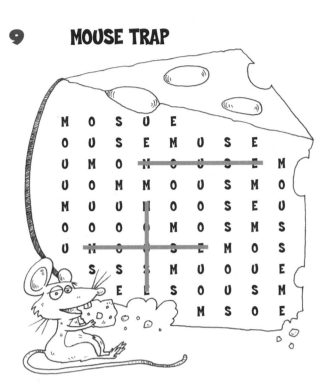

```
M O S U E
O U S E M U S E
U M O M O U S E M
U O M M O U S M O
M U U O O S E U
O O O M O S M U
U M O S E M O S
S S S M U O U E
E L S O U S M
M S O E
```

10   DESTINATION UNKNOWN

LISBON
LONDON
DUBLIN
HAVANA
VIENNA
WARSAW

11   RODEO RIDER

c

12   ON THE BALL

Volleyball

13   PENGUIN PARADE

i

14   A PRICKLY PROBLEM

c

16   TIME FOR A TRIP

Thailand, Barbados

17   CROSS EYED

14

18   BULLSEYE

a = 44
b = 34
c = 34

19 SUPERBAD
Krall the Conqueror

20 SETTING UP HOME
c, b, a

21 BEST IN SHOW
Here are some you might have thought of:
Sew, zip, press, rest, stir, strip, new, spit, swept, persist, wise, size, wet, rip, net

22 SWEET TREATS
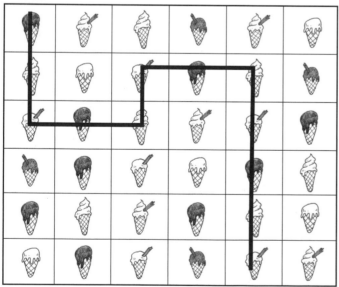

24 ALL TIME GREATS
1. Cycling
2. Fencing
3. Swimming
4. Athletics
5. Gymnastics

25 PERFECT PRIMATES
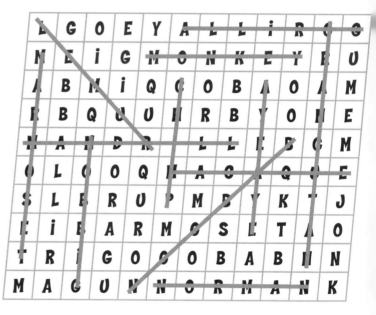

26 GONE IN A FLASH

e

27 PET PANDEMONIUM

8 pets are missing.

29 SHERIFF'S SUDOKU

30 SPORTS KIT

Boxing glove - boxing glove
Bowling ball - bowling pin
Helmet - bicycle
Cricket bat - stumps
Ice hockey stick - puck
Arrow - bow
Tennis ball - tennis racquet
Table tennis bat - ball

31 PAW PRINTS

Lion, wolf, skunk, lynx

32 COMIC STRIP

f, c, e, a, d, b

33 BRAIN TEASER

Carl owns a gerbil called Hector.
Susie owns a pony called Crystal.
Grace owns a cat called Peppa.

34 CHOCOHOLICS

35 SPOON SEARCH

There are ten spoons.

37 "C" CREATURES

Here are ten; did you think
of any more?
Camel, coyote, canary, crocodile,
cow, cheetah, cat, chimpanzee,
chicken, chameleon.

38 A COOL CLIMBER

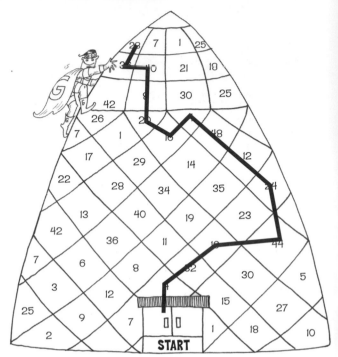

39 YOU CHOOSE

40 IN A STATE

The hidden state is Indiana.

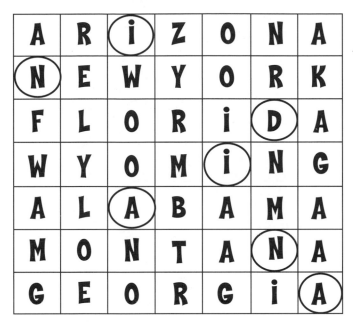

42 CROSS OUT

In case he got a hole in one

43 SAFARI TRAIL

45 A TRICKY QUESTION

Hercules

46 TRAIN TREK

1. 10:41
2. 7 hours 15 minutes
3. 16:35
4. The 19:45 from Paris is slowest.
5. 1 hour 55 minutes

47 SAY WHAT?
Saddle up and hit the trail.

48 EXTREME THRILLS
e

49 STINKY SUMS

50 ON THE MOVE
Mindreading

51 COLLARED
10

53 THE WILD WEST
1. E3
2. Groceries
3. The cemetery
4. C5

54 BOUNCE AROUND

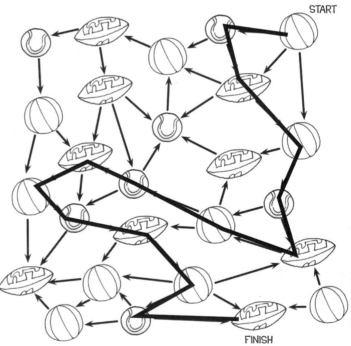

55 CRITTER LITTERS

53 - 46 = 7 (wild boar)

(12 x 12) - 132 = 12 (crocodile)

(9 x 9) - 80 = 1 (monkey)

45 ÷ 5 = 9 (wolf)

60 ÷ 12 = 5 (lion)

(8 x 6) ÷ 24 = 2 (polar bear)

56 FLYING HIGH

b

57 PET PUZZLER

58 CAUGHT ON CAMERA

59 BEHIND BARS

1 = 5

2 = 7

3 = 9

4 = 3

60 **ANYONE FOR TENNIS?**

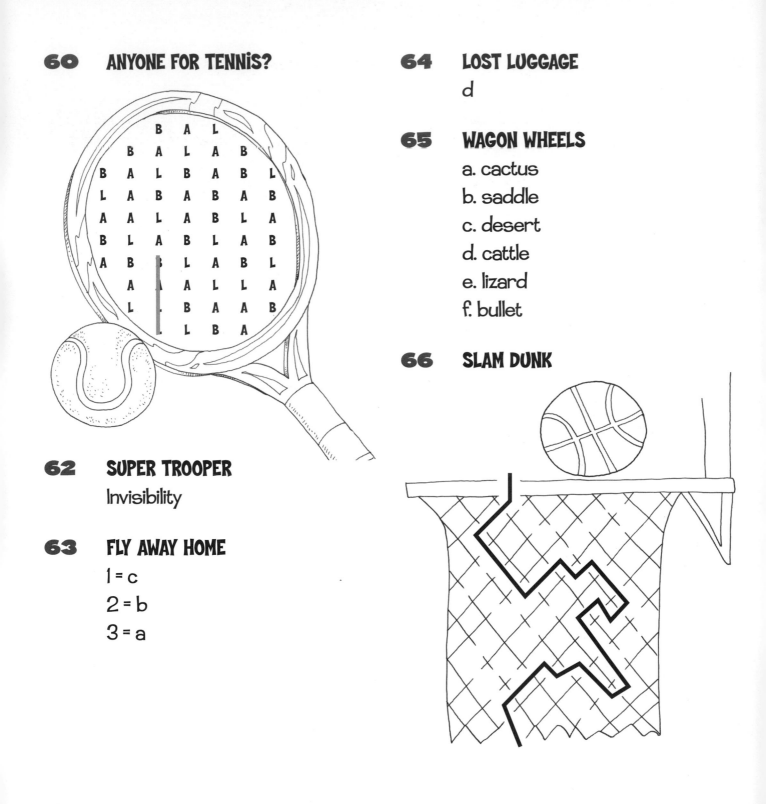

62 **SUPER TROOPER**
Invisibility

63 **FLY AWAY HOME**
1 = c
2 = b
3 = a

64 **LOST LUGGAGE**
d

65 **WAGON WHEELS**
a. cactus
b. saddle
c. desert
d. cattle
e. lizard
f. bullet

66 **SLAM DUNK**

67 LEAPING LEMURS!

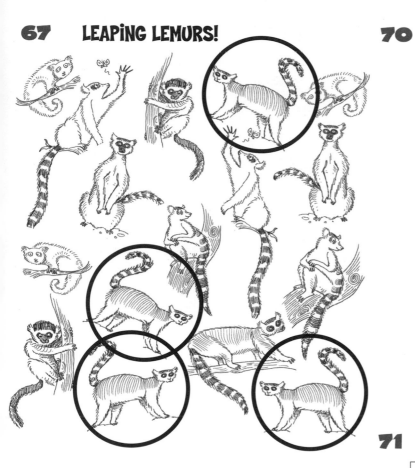

70 CYPRUS SUDOKU

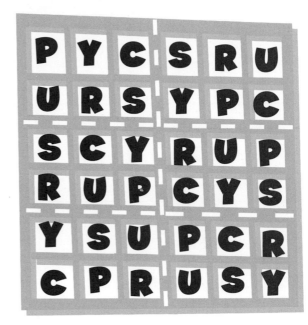

71 AMBUSHED!

68 SUPER SPELLINGS

Here are some you might have thought of:

Cover, selves, love, sir, cress, resolve, elves, lose, verse, cross, vile, serve, core, recess, veer, sole

72 PARK LiFE

1. D2
2. Archery
3. A3
4. C2
5. Tennis
6. D5

73 CUTE CUBS

d

74 ON THE RUN

Cape, gloves, boots, suit, mask, belt. The villain's name is Paradox.

75 NETTED

76 RiDiNG HiGH

78   STICK WITH IT
30

79   SSSSSSILLY SSSSSSTUFF
It got lockjaw

80   SUPER SHOOTERS
Strength

81   JUST JOKING
Because they have nine lives

82   CIAO ITALIA!
Pisa, Rome, Milan, Naples

83   POWWOW, NOW!
c

85   EAGLE EYES
a. D2
b. H8
c. G1
d. E6
e. A5
f. B2

86   BETTER, FASTER, HIGHER
a = 152
b = 151
c = 151

87   IT'S A MYSTERY

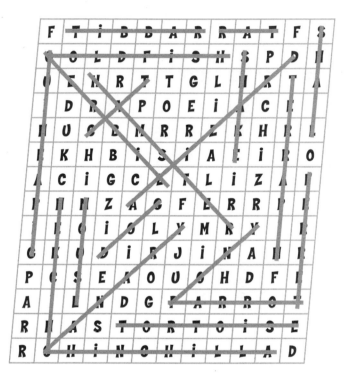

88   FUN IN THE SUN

89   PICK A POLE
g

90   BOWLED OVER
71

91   TIME TO EAT!
a = elephant
b = kangaroo

93   MUCKING OUT

94   ON THE CASE
1645

95   THE OLD WEST
Utah

96 ON YOUR BIKE
Cross country

98 JEWEL THIEF
The Jade Assassin

97 BIRD BRAINS

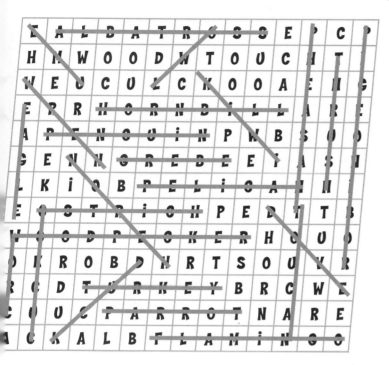

99 DOG TIRED

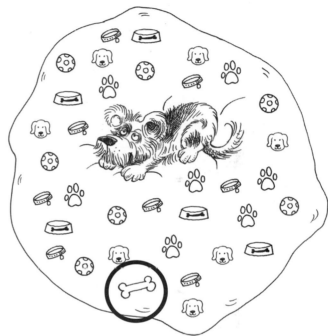

101 HOME, SWEET HOME
  a. D2
  b. B1
  c. B7
  d. E8
  e. H6
  f. E3

102 ALL THE BALLS

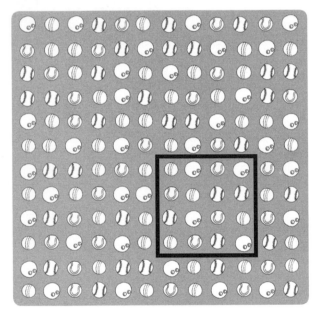

103 ROLL UP, ROLL UP!
  23

104 UNDERWATER RESCUE
  a and e

105 FUNNY BUNNIES
  e

106 DREAM TICKET
  Florida Keys

107 SADDLE UP

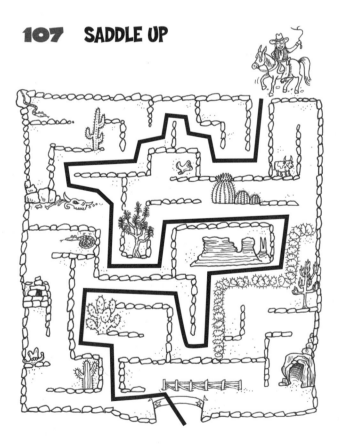

108   GOING FOR GOLD
Usain Bolt

110   BOO! HISS!
d

111   CUDDLY CREATURES
1. Peacock
2. A3
3. C4
4. E5
5. Piglets
6. Llamas

112   GET PACKING
The paired items are: flip flops, bucket (pail) and spade, face mask and snorkel, notepad and pen, toothbrush and toothpaste.

113   THE LONE RANGER

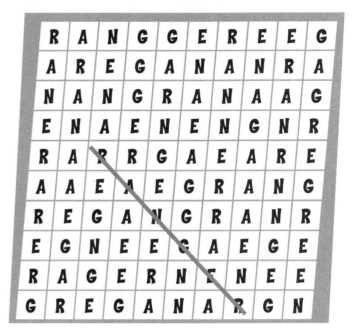

114   SPORTS SQUARE

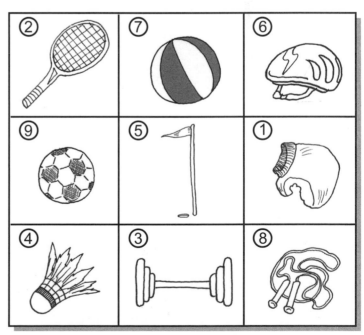

115 LION LAUGHS

He tasted funny

116 TO THE RESCUE!

There are ten party hooters.

118 LADY LIBERTY

e

119 THE SILVER SADDLE

a. D5
b. F2
c. C2
d. B7
e. H6
f. B8

120 COACH GOODWAY

f - he coaches gymnastics

122 HELP ME!

123 BIRD TALK

Australia

124 SNORKEL SCARE

e, f, a, c, b, d

126 WIN OR LOSE?

Because he kept drawing!

127 ICE, ICE BABY

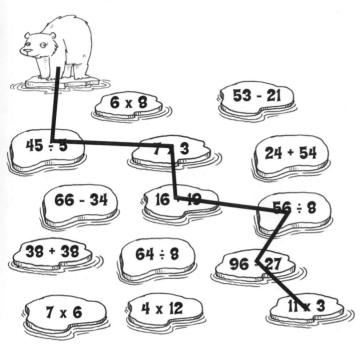

6 x 8

53 - 21

45 ÷ 5

7 x 3

24 + 54

66 - 34

16 - 10

56 ÷ 8

38 + 38

64 ÷ 8

96 - 27

7 x 6

4 x 12

11 x 3

128 SUPERFOODS
Blueberry pie

129 IT'S A STICK UP
12

130 MAKING CAMP
Amy is going to France
in a tepee.
Leigh is going to Spain
in a tent.
Millie is going to Italy
in a camper van.

131 OUTLAWED
They should look behind wild cat
mountain (D6).

133 ANIMAL MUDDLE!
Ferret, monkey, walrus, turtle,
weasel, beaver

134 STRANDED

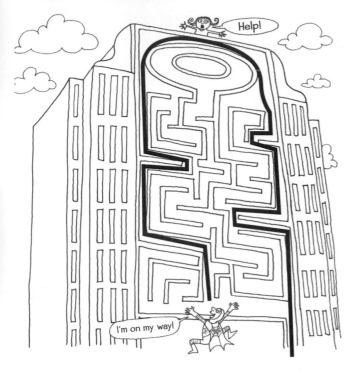

135 PUT IN THEIR PLACE

136 CITY SEARCH
Venice

137 CATCHING CATTLE
$24 \div 6 = 4$
$72 \div 8 = 9$
$48 \div 6 = 8$
$54 \div 9 = 6$
$45 \div 9 = 5$
$49 \div 7 = 7$

138 SPORTS SEARCH

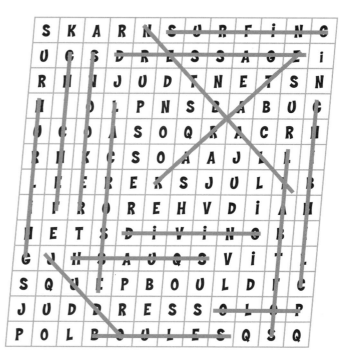

139 CREATURE COUNT
Butterflies = 15
Beetles = 10
Snakes = 6
Birds = 8

141 GO, GINNY, GO!

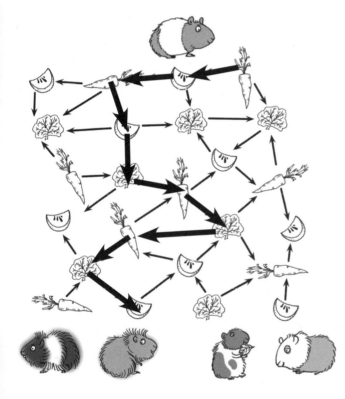

142 OFF WE GO!
Auckland, New Zealand
Athens, Greece
Toronto, Canada
Sydney, Australia
Bangkok, Thailand
Cairo, Egypt

143 BIRD'S EYE VIEW
b

144 SPORTS CAMP
a = climbing
b = canoeing

145 FOOTPRINTS

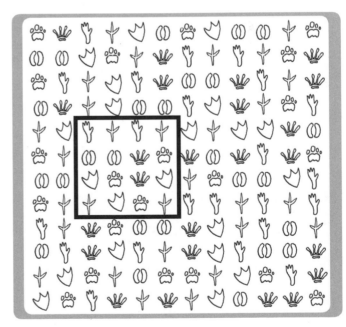

146   LASER LINES

151   A PRICKLY SITUATION

147   STABLE SHADOWS
d

149   YEE HA!
b and f

150   MUSCLE MAN
Wrestling

152   A BUSY DAY

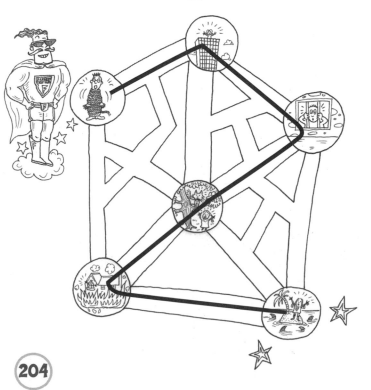

153 PETS ON PARADE
d

154 ROAD TRIP
Here are some you
might have thought of:
Big, snort, rot, hiss, stir, torn,
north, short, shirt, insist, boss,
hot, rib, right, tin, sob, night, orb,
thin, sit.

155 THE ACCUSED
a. D4
b. B6
c. E2
d. B3

156 MAKING A SPLASH

158 CHEMICAL CHAOS
BRAIN BLASTER, DISAPPEARIO,
MEGABELCH JUICE

160 LIBERTY LAUGHS
Because it can't sit down

161 CAUGHT OUT

162 SPORTS SUDOKU

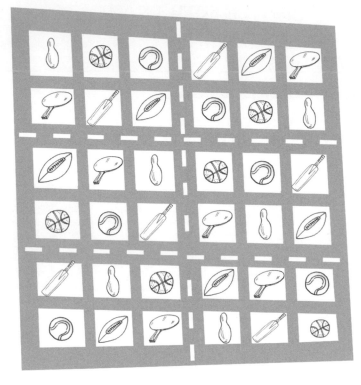

163 ENDANGERED SPECIES

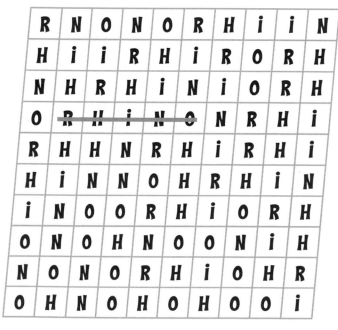

164 BLAST AWAY!

e

166 TOP TRIP

Sun, sea and sand

167 WANTED!

b

168 WINTER THRILLS

Curling, skating, luge, ski jump

169 OUT IN AFRICA

Lions

170 PARTY PROTECTOR

a. B2
b. G8
c. C7
d. D4
e. G2
f. B7

171 HAMSTER RUN

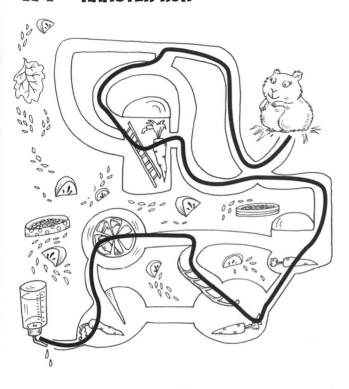

172 IT'S SNOW TIME!

174 STARTING BLOCKS
Individual medley

175 IN A FLAP
Humboldt

177 TANGLED UP

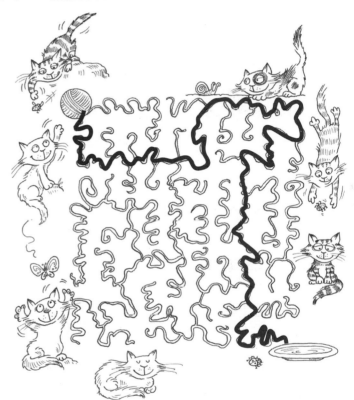

178 ISLAND DREAM

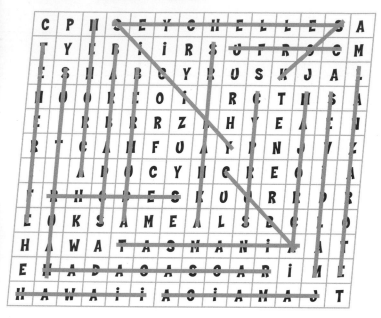

179 COWBOY TRAIL
8, 16, 24, 32, 40, 48, 56, 64, 72, 80, 88

181 RED ALERT
Borneo

182 UNMASKED!

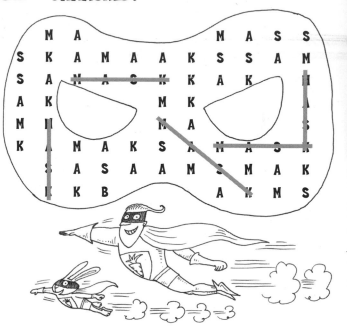